Medieval Costume

by Mistress Katrine de Baillie du Chat, O.L.

All artwork in this book was done by

Mistress Rodema de Rohan, OL.

Publisher's Note: This book is published by Raymond's Quiet Press for their friends in the Society for Creative Anachronism.

Second Printing, July, 1980.

Printed in USA.

Raymond's Quiet Press
6336 Leslie NE
Albuquerque, New Mexico 87109

ISBN 0-943228-01-8 5.25

DEDICATION

TO MISTRESS RODEMA DE ROHAN, without whose help, artistic skill, and encouragement this book would never have been finished.

AND

MISTRESS IRMINSUL THE IMPROBABLE, for her kindness, hard work, and unfailing good temper which set an example for us all.

BECAUSE

These two great ladies demonstrate so clearly that, no matter how fine her garb, a true lady's courtoisie and gentilesse are her finest adornments.

WITH THANKS FROM

Katrine

TABLE OF CONTENTS

Personagarb

In every time there have been some men and women who fit the fashion ideal, and others who simply had to make the best of whatever the style was. Luckily for SCA members, however, the Middle Ages provide more than a thousand years of changing garb from which any person can choose something appropriate and becoming to wear, fitted to his persona and looks.

The worst possible way to decide on a costume is to thumb through a superficial picture book like The Mode In Costume (cited because it is unfortunately ubiquitous in bad libraries everywhere) until you come to a pretty illustration, and then try to copy it line for line. Instead, you must consider the possible style from two points of view: your body and the rationale behind the design. Every type of garb has a certain set of rules on which it is based, including the fabrics available, the undergarments in use, the demands of modesty, the climate, and the circumstances under which it is to be worn, as well as the parts of the body to be ehphasized.

Thus if your choice is a Germanic or Anglo Saxon persona, your could not use a large-pattern borcade, velvet, or satin fabric even if the cut of the dress were accurate, since all these fabrics were invented later in time. If you want a fancy court costume, however, you could develop a connection with the Varangian guard or a Viking raider and use a patterned silk fabric of Byzantine type. It is almost always possible to find a substitute which will give you the effect you want if the first choice is inauthentic, but the total effect will be vastly better if you do enough research to find out the Correct substitute for the period. Again, you cannot create any fashionable post-1500's style (as opposed to peasant clothing) which looks anything but tacky - no matter what expensive outer fabric you use - without a real corset and farthingale (if needed) underneath, or expose a woman's forearm unless she is a launderess or whore. And, or course, you would not dress even a Viking persona in wool and furs for a summer tourney in al-Barran, an Egyptian anchorite in a homespun loincloth and bare feet for a Twelfth Night feast in Caerthe, or any persona in a velvet and satin court gown for a weekend at the Grand Outlandish.

Remember that in every period there were a wide variety of adaptations for each basic style, just as there are today. Most of the pictures which survive are of rich and important people wearing the most fashionable garb, which is why so many of the costumes look so cumbersome. But the various styles changed as they filtered down to the middle and lower classes, shedding hard-to-clean fabrics, decorative layers and details, inches of train and elaborate headdresses. Often a style which appears intimidating or bizarre in its extreme form, such a fifteenth century headgear or Elizabethan drum farthingales, can be made much easier and more comfortable in a peasant version. While high-fashion models are often tempting to seamstresses who want to produce a virtuoso display, and to dazzle the audience when they come off, they also provide many more ways to go wrong and look much worse when they fail. Simplicity (no pun intended) is often more effective. For example, one of the most beautiful and satisfying costumes I have ever seen was a simple Norman gown, a plain undecorated back-laced dress with straight sleeves. But the lady wearing it had the perfect figure type for the period and was absolutely authentic in every detail, form the cut of the dress and the silk casings on her long braids to her girdle and shoes.

Let me now turn to some specific medieval styles which are particularly good for certain figure types. The favored figure during most of the middle ages was the tall slim lord or lady, but not all of the styles demanded this. Very short ladies and lords should avoid the very enveloping fashions such as the houppelande or the sweeping-trained fifteenth century sideless surcotes and V-necked gowns. Simple vertical designs such as the Norman, Anglo-Saxon, or cotehardie are often effective for short ladies. Ladies of average height with small bust and larger hips can wear the houpplande, Tudor, loose ungirdled stypes such as thirteenth century or Byzantine, or fifteenth century garb, for during that century the fashionable figure had small breasts, a high waist, a full stomach, and wide hips - almost a pregnant look.

Ladies with slim figures and full bustlines can be absolutely smashing in an extreme low-cut cotehardie, Norman, or even bliaut, but they should avoid baggy styles like the Anglo-Saxon gown, the early sideless surcote, or the thirteenth century ungirdled "sack". For those however, who are generally heavy or alas! lumpy in the wrong places, these nightgown-like designs can hide many sins and lend much dignity. Full-busted, short-waisted ladies usually look best in the Italian Renaissance garb, which you may recall from films like Romeo and Juliet or Taming of the Shrew. Tall, thin ladies whose legs are their best features do have a problem, since every female medieval style is at least ankle length. Their most successful compromise is to choose a barbarian warrior-maid or Joan-of-Arc persona who can wear short male tunics and hosen. Slim, small ladies also seem to be the only ones who do not look shapeless and dumpy in Cavalier (Charles I) garb.

Lords have three basic effects to choose from in medieval garb: baronial (or martial), elegant, or sexy. Husky football player types (e. g. dwarves) often look good in fairly early fashions like Anglo-Saxon, Norse, or barbarian. If they choose later styles, they generally look better in simple tunics, surcotes, guardcorps, or long Byzantine-style robes. Nothing would be quite as incongruous as a Dwarf-sized lord trying to look at ease in an extreme courtrepy and long piked shoes. If a lord is very heavy or paunchy then full-length runics are the most effective. It is useless to attempt to disguise a heavy figure, and is more successful to create flamboyant, sweeping robes of the houppelande or Russian boyar kind, with long, flowing sleeves and lots of heavy trim, which give it an impressive and theatrical grandeur.

Tall, very thin lords should avoid any

styles shorter than knee length, and tend to appear at their best for court in somewhat full, floor-length robes with wide, decorated girdles. Young, slim lords should take advantage of the garb which shows off a good body. Among these are Italian Renaissance, the informal Elizabethan jerkin and hosen, and the cotehardie or its descendant the courtrepy (which can be as tight and short as courage permits). Short lords need not lack dramatic impact, as such noble gentles as Yang the Nausiating or Cariadoc of the Bow have demonstrated. They Should, however, pick uncluttered and fairly body-fitting garb such as barbarian, Arabic, or other tunic fashions which do not overwhelm them or create a fussy impression. Perhaps it seems odd that I have not recommended the more extreme dagged, dandified styles of the fifteenth century or the fantastic puffs and slashes of the German Renaissance. The reason is that very few modern men without stage training can handle themselves comfortably in dress that looks silly and un-masculine to them. However, if a lord can avoid acting and feeling self-conscious in such garb, he should be all means try it.

Making medieval clothes for children is great fun. Since they are small, two or three yards of fabric will make a complete outfit, and you can afford to experiment with exotic fabrics. With children, however, you must be careful to make sturdy, loose garb which can stand hard use, unless you want a special costume for court use only. Small children dressed in miniature fifteenth-century Little-Princess-In-The-Tower garb or Elizabethan pages' livery, or a tiny Tudor with a little farthingale can be exquisite as show pieces and really give children a sense of being important and a true part of the Society. If you are a family, it is certainly tacky to expend great care on the grown-ups garb and then stick the kids in a broadcloth tabard with a hole torn out for a neckline and tennis shoes. Think of the children's garb as a chance to practice on small amounts of fabric to avoid mistakes on large, expensive grown-up-sized costumes. For practical everyday tourney garb for children, the earlier types of T-shaped tunics are the most practical, knee length for boys and ankle-length for girls. Plain color cotton or flannel pajama bottoms make good braes for barbarian costumes, and for most other periods it is simplest to use s sturdy heavy-weight tights, with or without shoes. Bedroom slippers which fit the foot fairly closely are often good approximations of medieval shoes for children, and are generally fairly cheap. Cotton baby kimonoes or "saques" make good undertunics for children up to three or so years old, and babies can wear them alone. In the medieval period, babies, of course were generally swaddled, but long (and often elaborate) gowns were used for christenings and important events.

In most periods of the middle ages, children's clothes were mainly miniatures of their parents' dress. The main differences for girls are that they did not wear headdresses, or (usually) heavy corsets or farthingales, and their clothes were (usually) simpler in cut than the extreme adult versions. There are exceptions; think of Valasquez's unhappy-looking little Infantas in immoble adult-style garb. Girls must, however, cover their forearms. For boys there are few differences except that, for practical reasons, they are usually more comfortable in knee-length tunics and they should not bear steel (or worse yet, imitation swords of plastic - Yeech how awful!) until they can handle it responsibly. Since few boys now-a-days get a horse of their own or go to another household for fostering as a page, it can be a true mark of reaching responsible age to give a boy a real but dull dagger at seven or eight years old, as a sign he is becoming a grown-up boy. Teach him respect for real steel early and he will handle it responsibly when he comes of age to bear a sword (steel <u>or</u> rattan). For the sixteenth and seventeenth centuries, remember that boys were not "breeched" until about seven years old, and before that wore long dresses exactly like their sisters.

The final aspect of SCA garb which must be considered is accessories, expecially headdresses. Ladies, remember that unless you are under twelve years old, a virgin bride, or a queen in coronation robes, YOU MUST WEAR A HEADDRESS. To appear otherwise was not only uncouth but obcene in medieval eyes, and not even the poorest peasant woman showed herself in public without a rag to cover her hair. This does not mean that the headdress must be heavy, bulky, or elaborate. It may be no more than a string of pearls wound artisticly in the tresses or a wreath of fresh flowers. If you have long, thick hair (lucky you) it can be shown to good advantage in a number of styles: long Norman plaits, thirteenth century ramshorns, or the fantastic hairstyles of the Italian Renaissance. If you hair is covered, it can be with only a light veil or circlet which augments without concealing. If you are not particularly concerned with displaying your hair or if it is short, you have a wide variety of options. The simple rectangular or circular veil can be wrapped around the head and shoulders in a number of ways, and will go with almost any period style; a wimple and barbe was worn even in the fifteenth century by widdows. Thirteenth and fourteenth century styles are mainly neat, simple headdresses like little templars and snoods (drispines) which are easy to make and light to wear.

For those with more elaborate ambitions, there are the wonderful romantic creations of the fifteenth century and Renaissance: henins, reticulated hoods, heart-shaped headdresses, gable and French hoods, and more. The only caution in dealing with these styles is the same as the one I mentioned in connection with the more elaborate costume styles which go along with them. Be sure you can carry out the design completely, for a badly done henin (of which there are far too many among those who have the delusion that "fairy princess" is an authentic style) is far more obvious than a badly done headrail.

Lords have less need for headwear, since they were often bare-headed or encased in helmets. But in the later centuries, there are many male court costumes which really look incomplete without some sort of hood or hat. The simplest to make is the basic hood and its adaptation, the chaperon. Several kinds of mundane hats and caps can be adapted quite easily to look like styles you see in period pictures. It is hard to give specific advice on headgear because most costumes are closely allied with a particular type of hat or headdress and the headgear really depends on the style of garb chosen.

We have now come full circle, and returned to the costume book where we began. Once you have chosen the basic style and period of fashion which is best fitted to you, then look at all the illustrations you can, and especially read several good general references to find out what the rationale behind your own style was, and what accessories it needs to complete it. For this the two best single references I know are Herbert Norris's four volume Costume and Fashion and Cunnington's series of Handbooks on costume by centuries.

Evolution of Fabric in the Middle Ages

One thing which will become obvious after a little study of medieval fabric is that, for all practical purposes, it is not possible to find modern material which reproduces that of the period exactly. As Mary Fernald writes in Costume Design and Making (page 11):

"It is, of course, impossible to reproduce exactly the materials that were in common use hundreds of years age, for the methods of weaving were utterly different from those in use today, even though the principle of warp and woof is basically the same. For instance, it is today impossible to obtain a velvet that is similar in texture to the old short-pile velvet of even so recent a date as 1870. The nearest approach to this in modern material is millinery velvet lacks completely the rigidity of Victorian velvet, which did, literally, almost stand by itself. The velvet of 1870 was, of course, machine made just as is your velvet today, but with a change of taste in material, except at great cost, it is impossible to repeat the texture of sixty years ago; how much more impossible, therefore, it is for us to repeat the texture of material which were hand-woven. Another difficulty which presents itself to designers is the question of colouring. It is possible to fake the texture of a material to a certain extent by the careful choice of materials and use of linings to give stiffness or weight, but is impossible to fake colours. Up to about the middle of the nineteenth century all dyes were non-mineral in origin. Since the middle of the nineteenth century all dyes have been aniline, that is mineral dyes, and now it is impossible to obtain any material in the open market, with the exception of Harries and Donegal tweeds, which are not aniline dyed, with the result that bright colours tend to have a certain crudeness, whilst some colours such as a clear, cold yellow are almost impossible to obtain.

The old dyes, though bright, were invariably soft and therefore a greater variety of color combinations was possible than is the case today with cruder dyes".

So we are effectively forced to choose the modern fabric which is the **closest** to period material. There are traps, too, in wait for the unwary, for a number of fabric names have come down to us intact while the materials they refer to have altered so much as to be unrecognizable. A good example is taffeta, which is now a flimsy, cheap fabric with a shiny surface, but was at one time thick, heavy silk with a soft nap, worthy to be used in royal clothing. Queen Anne, wife of Henry VIII had a fabulously expensive bedgown of black velvet lined with taffeta of this type.

All medieval fabric, of course, was of natural origins. Wool and linen of various manufacture were the most common in Europe since they were produced locally. Cotton was brought from India originally and later grown in Egypt. Since it was imported it was rare; a garment of cotton caused a sensation in Byzantium in the fifth century, and there is a record of Charlemange appearing in a wool undertunic with a cotton overgarment (The Dawn of European Civilization). The most prestigous fabric, from ancient time through the Middle Ages, was silk, which was imported at first from China by means of the long Arab trade routes.

With these four fibers, plus leather and furs, the Middle Ages created a wide variety of

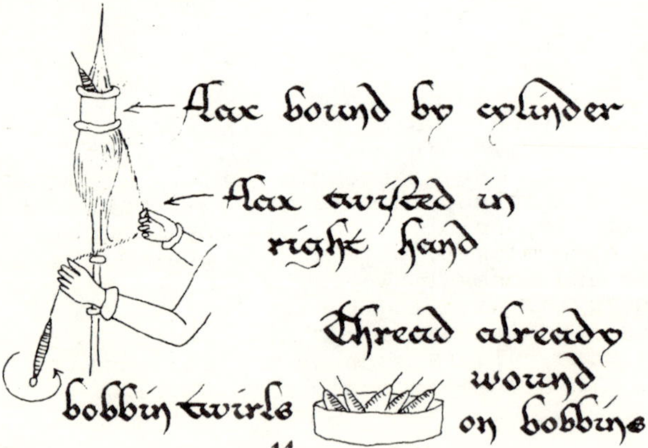

materials as styles changed and textile technology developed. The Celts in the time of the Roman Empire (described by Pliny) used cloth of wool and flax "of the texture of thick coarse felt, and some of much finer make (Norris, p. 9) dyed in purple, scarlet, yellow, blue, green brown, and especially red.

Cloaks were virtually always red, a characteristic retained by isolated Celtic peoples such as the Bretons until well into the Norman period. The Celts were fond of patterned cloth, striped (later called "rayed"), spotted, and checked. The check was either woven into the fabric or created by sewing many small squares together like patchwork.

The Teutons had a considerable effect on design in clothing in the early medieval period, by introducing the braies (or long pants) and short tunic which became usual for informal wear throughout Europe. Their fabric, however, was the same rather coarse hempen linen and woolen cloth, combined with fur. Most of this fabric was in natural colors decorated with embroidery, applique, and rarely woven-in design in bright primary colors. Since "natural" and "homespun" fabric has become popular in the mundane world in the last few years, there is a much wider range of current fabrics to imitate this early garb. Heavy gauze, some kettlecloth, "linen-look" fabric, heavy unbleached muslin, real or imitation wool or wool flannel (sometimes called "school-boy flannel" or suiting flannel) are good possibilities. Some sturdy people use burlap for peasant clothing, but this does tend to be rather undomfortable. These fabrics lend themselves wonderfully to large-scale embroidery with floss or yarn in bright colors. Other good decorations are fur or lengths of tablet weaving-type trim. The Teutons were far from crude in their artistic efforts, as a glance at Gothic jewlry will show, but very delicate trim tends to look out of place on these rough fabrics.

From the fifth to at least the twelfth centuries, Byzantium remained the source of court protocol, fashion, and elegant cloth,

6th Century Patterns

riveled to a degree by the Arab world after the Crusades. The Empire retained some of the weaving methods of the Roman period, and in the early centuries western kings imported rich fabrics such as silk brocade or damask which could not yet be produced at home. Weaving was somewhat more advanced in England than on the Continent during the Anglo-Saxon period because a few Greek weavers emigrated there, and raw silk and metalic thread were used. Embroidery, mainly of Byzantine design was quite advanced in England, the beginning of the English fame in this area which was to reach its peak in the much-prized Opus Anglicum of the thirteenth century.

In the year 551, two persian monks succeeded in smuggling some silkworm eggs out of China and returning with them to Byzantium, which continued to monopolize the manufacture of silk in Europe for the next six hundred years. It was made into many different fabrics. Sou Twan (Chinese) or Samit was a closely woven, thick rich silk whose name eventually became "satin" and "samite". The earlier version was not so high in lustre, for bridal satin as we know it did not cme into use before the late sixteenth century. Plain-colored heavy silk of this kind was used for the Imperial paludamentum or Mantle of State and other ceremonial garments.

Patterned silks were produced in the West from the fifth century AD in Persia, Syria, Egypt and the Empire. They included damask in which the pattern was of the same color as the ground but woven as to look darker or lighter in tone, and brocade which could be multi-colored, and was "a weft and a woof of silk, sometimes intermixed with gold or silver, on which a pattern was superimposed by an independent weaving with the shuttle". (Norris, p. 212). Many Byzantine Brocades were woven with circles covering the ground, each circle containing one or more styalized figures of animals. Other silk materials of the early Middle Ages were Boquerant or Bougram, a fine supple fabric probably something like cashmere with camel or goat hair mixed with silk and threads of gold or silver used to form stripes or geometrical figures. Baudekyn had a weft of gold and woof of silk, producing a beautiful shot (changeable) fabric either plain or patterned, and cendal was a silk thinner than samite whether striped or plain colors. These latter two were known in the East in the ninth or tenth century but not the West until the twelfth or thirteenth. Gauze was used from the tenth century. It was a transparent thin silk fabric, sometimes shot with gold, somewhat like chiffon or even the sparkling translucent fabric called glitter organza in modern stores.

Byzantine costume was essentially static in design, with minor variations, so that the primary focus was on elaboration of the fabrics and decoration. The clavii or bands down the front of the tunic, the segmentae (isolated designs) and borders were woven or embroidered in gold and encrusted with jewels or metal. Often the cloth itself was all or partly of gold metal. Byzantine dyers, and following them, the Merovingians, favored strong color - scarlet, purple. gold, deep blue, salmon: often three or four colors were combined in one costume. The Anglo-Saxon sometimes followed this fashion but in

A Typical 13th century pattern

general, especially in the lower classes, tended toward softer shades and colors such as grey, dull green, brown, and natural. Color was concentrated in the border decoration, which was usually of simple geometric forms, triangles, diamonds, squares, and circles. Celtic decoration was more loose in form, although its construction was quite exact. It was made of endlessly looping and recrossing lines called Celtic Knowwork.

The twelfth and thirteenth centuries marked the division between the early and middle Middle Ages, mainly resulting from the wider trade, higher expectations, and advancing technology (agriculture as well as mechanical) associated with the period of the Crusades. How much of this was caused by, or directly resulted from, the Crusades themselves has been a hotly debated subject and I will ignore it here. However, cloth manufacture made an advance at about this time, as it did again with the next major era of expansion in the late sixteenth and early seventeenth centuries. Silk fabrics which appeared in this period included Frize (a cloth of gold), creped silk (like Crepe-de-cine), sarsenet, siglaton (similar to cut velvet) and taffeta. Another fabric made like velvet but of cotton was called pell, and can probably be imitated very well by ribless courderoy. A very fine, gauze-like linen called cambric was popular for undergarments and veils. This stuff came to be called chainsil in the Norman period and lawn in the High Middle Ages, an indespenisble foundation to the changing outer costume until the Elizabethan era and beyond. Wool was sometimes treated in the same way to make a soft fabric like fine cashmere.

The various fabrics used for overgarments in the medieval period were usually heavier than modern dress fabric, although they were often not at all stiff. Most pictures show long garments lying on the ground in thick, heavy folds. So most modern fabric will require lining to hang and drape properly. As with any general statement, of course, there are exceptions; one was the bliaut, which was a style of about 1130-1150 made of very fine fabric pleated in knife-like folds like an old-fashioned squaw dress skirt.

By the twelfth century the influence of Byzantium was waning and the production for most cloth was local in Europe itself. Figure fabric was woven in pictures for use as wall hangings in France, made of wool, silk, gold, and silver. Patterned fabric for clothing was also produced, called semee or diaper if it was all-over design. Now began the long partnership between England as an exporter of high-quality wool and the Low Countries where the wool was converted into cloth. Some plain cloth was produced in England itself, especially since a number of Flemish weavers emigrated to England soon after the Conquest. The common people, as was usually everywhere, wore homespun of linen, wool, or linsey-woolsey. The length of the Yard measure for cloth (called an ell at the time) was set by Henry I, who used his own arm as a measure, and broadcloth was set by law at two ells width by Richard I. At this time broadcloth referred only to this width, not the type of material.

New fabrics which were used during this central period included fustian of linen warp and cotton woof with a surface of short sheered pile, similar to the pell mentioned earlier. It was used for everyday dress by all classes, and when the fabric was worn, the nobility would send their clothing out to have it reshorn. Russet was a coarse homespun; it was sometimes dyed brown with bark but was often natural, for the name did not yet have any connection with the color of the fabric. Herbert Norris believes that knitting was used, probably for hose, possibly for clothing, at this time, but this is a disputed point. Bands of woven decoration, often very rich and elegant, were

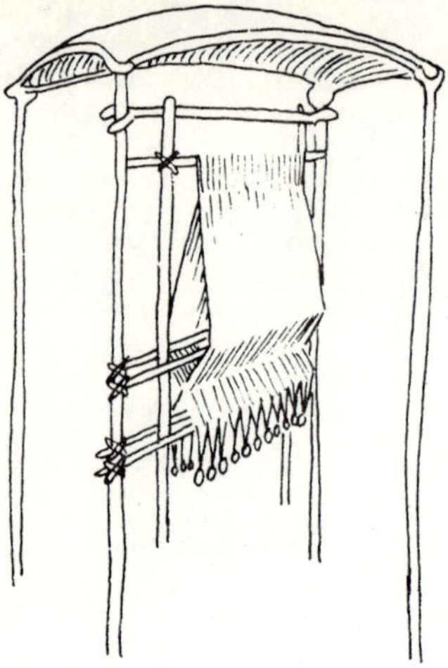

A vertical 13th century loom erected under a permanent roof

called passementerie. Esclarte was a very high-quality woolen cloth, mainly in scarlet, often used for state garments, and perse was a similar blue cloth. Lyraigne was a woolen cloth of a light "cobweb" texture. Cotton was used to make padding for gambesons worn under armor, and fabrics like muslin and dimity.

The High Middle Ages, the fourteenth and fifteenth centuries, brought an entirely new type of garment, fitted tightly to the body like the cotehardie and V-necked gown. Where previously splendor had resulted from the graceful drape and expense and beautiful design of fabric, fashion now required expert cut and tailoring of the garment as well. Fabric had to withstand more stress. Edward III and Queen Philippa established a colony of Flemish weavers in England in the mid-fourteenth century, and cloth began to be manufactured in specialized districts. Wool worsted (formerly called saye), came from the village of that name, baize from Sudbery, frieze from Wales, fustian from Norwish, serge from Colchester and Taunton, kersey, a coarse form of saye, from

Devon, and so on. The great trade with Flanders, and lesser trade with other fabric-producing areas such as Italy, declined. England and Holland embarked on a period of violent rivalry still reflected in such linguistic fossil terms of abuse as "Dutch treat", "Dutch courage", "Dutch Uncle", and so on.

New materials appearing at about this time included *bourde*, a striped eastern stuff, a type of cloth of gold called *aurem in serico*, cashmere or *cameline*, *carda*, a soft, fluffy cotton like swansdown used for lining, *cottum*, a wooly stuff from the fur of cats and dogs, *flannen* or flannel, and *marbrinus*, a silk woven for the lower classes. The three fabrics which were to be the mainstay of aristocratic garb for the next three centuries came into their own at this time: velvet, satin, and *tissue* of light-weight cloth of gold. In the next century the quality of some cloth, such as worsted, improved, but little in the way of new invention occurred. Cloth of gold was woven in blue, white, crimson, green, and purple, and velvet became more common. A new term for gold trim, woven or knotted, was "venice gold".

A 13th century shoe showing a typical fabric design

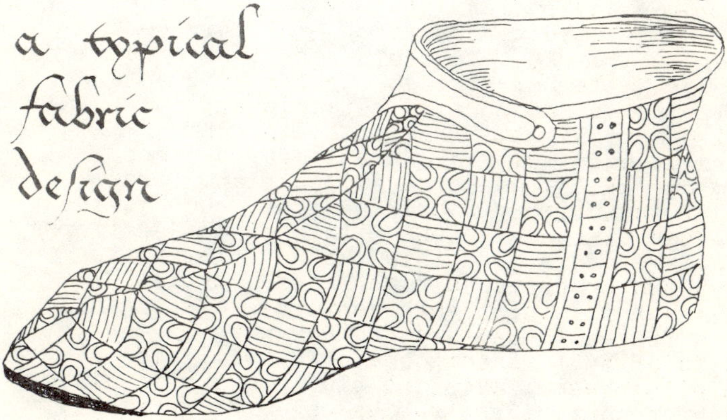

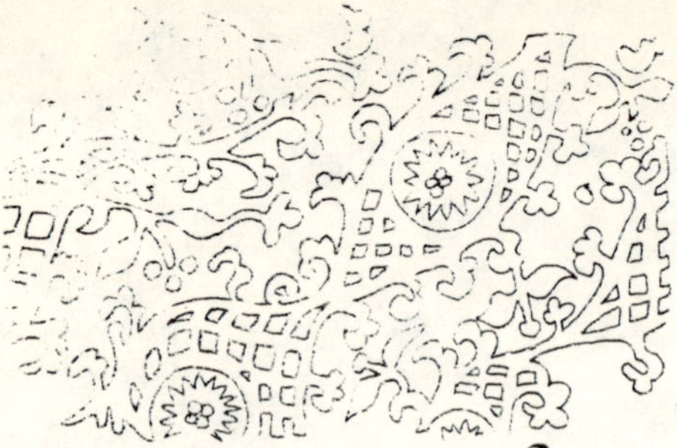

A 15th century brocade

Fur became gradually more popular through the fourteenth and fifteenth centuries, as trim or lining. "Fur" was originally a verb meaning "to line with" someting. The most valuable furs were sable, ermine, miniver, or ermine without the black tails, and vair, made of the white ermine and the pelt or a grey squirrel called gris sewn together in a pattern (This fur became a heraldic ground). Other popular furs were martin, rabbit, beaver, and budge or lambskin.

Color and pattern are always the hardest elements of garb to describe. The thirteenth century and early fourteenth were fond of small all-over patterns, stripes running horizontally, vertically, or diagonally heraldic applique, and parti-colordesigns. The fifteenth century tended toward considerably larger all-over designs based on scrolling and styalized plant forms. Some of the drapery fabric designs, such as the styalized pinecone shapes within diamond-patterns of foliage, come from this period. The State shoe shown on previous page shows a typical pattern of the thirteenth century. Also detail from a fifteenth century brocade worn by the Duchess of Bedford composed of a vermillion design with green leaves and blue stars with diamonds for centers and rubies used for berries beneath the leaves. (Shown above). In the four-

Pine Pattern brocade 15th cent.

teenth centuries, colors became more and more sophisticated, although the nomenclature lacked the panache of such Elizabethan colors as goose-turd-green. The fifteenth century prefered soft, pastel and "off" colors such as rose, cream, mauve, violet, sky-blue, blue-green as well as the traditional heraldic colors: gules, vert, sable, azure, or purpure, and argent which were used in the heraldic decorations on garb. Some color names of the later Middle Ages are listed below, taken from Norris:

aurnola	- orange	jaune	- bright yellow
brun	- brown	meaereon	- rose-purple
cendre	- dark grey	murrey	- deep claret
cramoisy	- crimson	paonace	- peacock

garance	- madder	plunket	- medium blue
graine	- cochineal red	celestyne	- sky blue
herbal	- brown-green	verdulet	- bright blue-green

Velvet was the most fashionable fabric of the early Tudor period, almost always in deep, warm tones like black, burgundy, gold, brown, scarlet, and deep green. Underskirts, sleeves, doublets, and other secondary articles of clothing were often of plain-color satin, damask, brocade, or cut velvet. Some of these fabrics were of soft shades like cream or the elegant blue-grey in one famous portrait of Henry VIII from 1542. These materials were often figured in rather rigid designs based on plant forms or Celtic interlace patterns, on a massive scale. Cloth of gold and silver also played a great part, for the clothing of the period was splendid and bombastic. Some tissue had a damask pattern, some was shot with a color of silk, and some were made like velvet with a gold ground and colored pattern or vice versa.

Pomegranate Pattern - Catherine of Aragon's Badge - 16th c.

The lawn used for undergarments was much more visible, peeping out at neck and wrists and through the slashes, puffs, pinkings, and tied-on sleeves.

This period saw the second major change in the weaving industry; a loom of the time is shown below. Basic weaving moved out of the towns to escape the rigid control of the guilds, and was put out on a piece-work basis in the country. More elaborate cloth was now created by large (in medieval terms)"factories" of master-clothiers who employed large numbers of specialized craftsmen in some fourteen operations which were required to produce a finished piece of fabric. Most of the materials produced were similar to those mentioned before: strong woolen worsted (lasting, russels), coarse linen (dowlas), and combinations of these fibers for the poor. Many of the same fabrics continued in use, like saye, russet, frieze, kersey, etc. Some new ones were lockram, a linen, grograine, a piled fabric, blanket, whence the name of the bedcover, bombazine frisado, a better-quality wool fabric, rugges, a fuzzy rough cloth, and many others.

A 15th century horizontal loom

We have a much more complete list of fabric names for this and later periods because so many of the wardrobe accounts and wills which list garments have come down to us. The older fabrics continued in use by the upper classes as well. Other than lawn almost all of them had at least some silk, including velvet, satin, taffeta, damask, brocade, and tinsel.

The main changes of the elizabethan period were the introduction of mirror satin, which was like modern slipper satin, and the first wide use of lace of the modern kind as opposed to cut and drawn work. Colored embroidery in representational figures was highly valued and used to cover large areas of garments as it had not been for several centuries. In part this was due to the growing fondness for satin over velvet and lighter shades, although scarlet and black continued to be popular. The most peculiar subjects were used for costume embroidery, including unprepossessing animals like spiders, snails, frogs, flies, and worms, and odd symbolic things such as eyes and ears on one of Elizabeth's dresses to represent her vigilence. However, birds, plants, and animals in highly naturalistic style, were also important motifs. The lack of restraint of the embroiderers is exemplified by the coat of arms issued to the Broiderers' Guild of London in the year of Elizabeth's accession: "paly of six argent and azure, on a fesse gules; between three lions passant gardant or, two broches in saltier, between two trundles or, Crest, on a wreath, a dove displayed argent, encircled with gold all proper. Supporter, two lions or, gutee de sang". With all this, they had a motto, too!

The age was a pushy one; very many cheap fabrics were made to imitate expensive ones, such as stammel and velure, which looked like escalarte and velvet respectively, and cheap imitation taffeta of linen. The manufacturers also indulged in many fraudulent practices to gull social climbers such as gumming cheap velvet to give it the weight and stiffness of the real material.

The colors of the Elizabethan England were delightful. Some of the more delicate shades were imported, but mention was made as early as 1534 of regulation of dyers producing brown, blue, pink, tawney, and violet. New colors included incarndine (flesh color), and migraine (pomegranate red) among the reds. The most subtile color variations were now possible; for example, just one tapestry woven in 1548 called for no less than eight thousand different shades! One interesting color was "Isabella". The Queen of Castile was besieged by the Moors, and vowed not to change her shift until the siege was lifted. When it was, nine months later, the shift had aquired the shade afterward known by her name. Among the most unusual color names were clodie-color (grey), dead Spaniard, Devil in the Hedge, goose-turd green, ladies' blush, lustie gallant, popingay, and a variant of dead Spaniard called Espagnol malade - no doubt a lighter shade, since he hadn't expired yet.

By the end of the Elizabethan period, almost any modern fabric and color can be used, as long as modern patterns are avoided. Knit silk is documented for use in stockings by this time, but not for general garb. Fabrics ranged from stiff velvet and thick silk to filmy veiling and lace, and everything in between. While techniques of manufacture changed with the coming centuries, we have little reason to believe that Elizabethan fabrics have yet been surpassed except in washability.

All illustrations are redrawn from Norris, unless noted.

Bibliography

Bellerophon Books Henry VIII & His Wives, San Francisco.

Fernald, Mary. Costume Design and Making, London, Adam and Charles Black, 1973.

Hill, Margot and Bucknell, Peter. The Evolution of Fashion, London, BT Batsford Ltd. 1967.

Norris, Herbert. Costume and Fashion. 4 volumes, J. M. Dent and Sons, London, 1927.

Plummer, John. The Hours of Catherine of Cleves, New York, George Braziller.

Rice, David Talbot. The Dawn of European Civilization, New York, McGraw-Hill, 1965.

And Many Others In Passing.

from a 10th century minature

Byzantines & Barbarians

The two major influences on dress in the period 500-1100 AD were Byzantium and the Germanic tribes of Northern Europe. There was some contact with Eastern tribes such as the Huns, the Arabs, and the Far East, but their influence on western costume was not great.

Upper-class Byzantine costume is difficult to imitate successfully, not because it is hard to construct (it is a basic T-tunic in cut) but because it was liberally encrusted with jewels and gold, often made of richly brocaded fabric, and decorated with elaborate accessories. Because the design was largely static, the nobility concentrated on decoration and 'extravagant tendencies which, increasing during the following centuries, were to culminate in the eleventh century in a wild orgy of sartorial magnificance". (Norris I, p. 147).

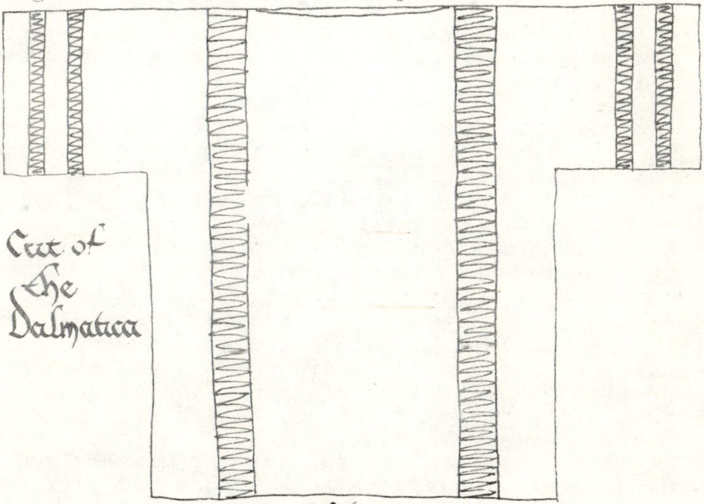

Cut of the Dalmatica

The basic garment was the tunica, which had been the common undergarment of the Romans. Then it had been white with two bands of color down the front and back, which originally meant membership in the equestrian order but later became purely decorative. The sleeves were short at first, but by the end of the Roman period had become wrist-length. Over the tunica was worn the <u>dalmatica</u>, which, as the name indicates, was at first an oriental garment from Dalmatia. It was the quintessential T-tunic: a long piece of fabric folded in half with an opening left for the head at the fold and the sides sewn up in an inverted "L" shape to form wide sleeves. This remained the basic method of construction for all garments until about the thirteenth century. The decorative bands were transferred to the dalmatica from the tunica, and the two types were merged, the only difference being the shape of the sleeves. The outer garment was now decorated with borders at the hem, wrists, and neckline, and with separate squares or circles of embroidery or decoration, called <u>segmentae</u> on each side of the front above the hem and on the shoulders. From the third to the sixth centuries, this decoration was usually woven into the garment by the method known as "tapestry darning" in dull purple, blue, red, green and yellow.

Over this was worn the formal mantle called the <u>paludamentum</u>. It became more and more elaborate, graduating from plain color heavy silk to gold embroidery and pearls to rich brocades covered with jewels. On the front and back left of this mantle along the open edge was a rectangular segment of decoration, always the most elaborate part of the garment, called the <u>tablion</u>.

Late Roman shaded imperceptibly into Byzantine. The Eastern (and Western) royalty and nobility of the fifth century wore the tunic and mantle just described, the tunic only knee-length, with bare legs and open shoes still closely resembling sandals. The sixth century saw the introduction of leg coverings. Roman upper classes adopted tight-fitting stockings called <u>hosa</u>. The full pants or trousers, called <u>bracco</u>, remained Germanic costume not often worn in the Empire; they were regarded as "abominable and disgusting garments so long associated with depraved savages". (Norris I, P. 156). The two bands of decoration down the front had now shrunk to waist length, and gradually crept upward until they merged with the neckline border.

Wearing the Lorum

Another garment which became established at this time was the lorum, a long scarf nine to twelve inches wide by eighteen feet long. It had once been a version of the toga worn by consuls as a badge of office. By this time it had become only a decorative strip of rich fabric, often gorgeously adorned with gold, jewels, and pearls. The picture shows the way it was worn. It became an item of court costume very popular from the eighth to the twelfth centuries. Sometimes, the lorum was made as a wider strip with a hole in the middle for the head and was worn like a scapular. This was also the shape of the ecclesistical pallium which was given by the Pope as a sign of special favor. Shoes also began to assume the typical medieval shape of a closed short boot or slipper rather than a sandal.

Hairdressing for men remained fairly static throughout the Byzantine period, from 400 to 1200 AD. It was a round bowl cut curled under all around the head like a short pageboy, brushed out in all directions from the crown in a radiating circle that reached to the nape of the neck in back. Men's faces were generally clean-shaven until about the ninth century when beards and mustaches became the fashion among sober and important nobles. Young men often remained bare of chin. These beards were short and neatly trimmed with a rounded bottom shape.

By the eighth century it had become the fashion for important noblemen to wear ankle-length tunics, a wide-sleeved dalmatica over a tight-sleeved undergarment, the outer one decorated with wide bands of embroidery at the hem, neckline, and upper arm. Patterned silks, both brocade and damask, were now well developed and were used either alone or decorated over the pattern with further designs of embroidery and jewels. One good example of this style which has survived is known as "Charlemagne's dalmatic" and was probably a gift from a manufacturer in Byantium. It has figures of Christ and the saints in a highly realistic style embroidered completely over an underlying brocade. Very heavy borders, especially at neck and hem are one of the most outstanding features of Byzantine style. This type of court dress continued without major change until the fall of Constantinople to the Latin Crusaders. As before, however, the short tunic continued to be worn by young men and ordinary citizens.

One interesting group within the Byzantine population was the Varangiam Guard, the Emperor's personal bodyguard, who swore an oath ("var") to him. Vladimir the Great of Russia (980-1015) had transferred their liege-oath from himself to Basil II of the Empire. They wore their own native costume: a short sleeveless tunic called a "kyrtil" with above it a shorter tunic of skin ("hjup")and a "byrnja" or byrnie of ring-mail on top. The legs were covered by cross-gartered bracco, and the feet by simple leather shoes of the sort found in excavations of the Bog People. For ceremonial occasions, these guards wore the famous helms with horns popularly associated with Vikings. Due to this influence, some Byzantine civilians are seen wearing bracco of the same kind, but this was rare.

Typical Male attire in the late Byzantine period

For the last few centuries of Byzantine existence, the thirteenth through fifteenth centuries, the dress of the nobility in the east and west was fairly similar, except for the Byzantine use of the lorum, worn only rarely (and only by Holy Roman Emperors) in the west. The basic dress continued to be a long-sleeved undertunic, long or knee-length, with one or more wider-sleeved overtunics above it. The paludamentum had been exchanged for a semi-circular cloak with the tablion elongated into a decorative border. The Frankish pedules, sock-like short boots, had been imported, and for the first time a type of hat became popular. This was either a sort of stocking cap or Phrygian cap, or a hat with a round, high crown, sometimes cone-shaped, with a stiff turned-up brim. The more elaborate version was almost exactly like the headdress worn by Russian Orthodox high churchmen-round and high, with a stiff band around the forehead.

Women's Dress

Women's dress of Byzantium also, of course, evolved from the late Roman, but became increasingly similar to men's as the centuries wore on, the main difference being in the headdress. The fifth century style included an undertunic with long, tight sleeves, then an overgarment called the stola (although it bore little resemblence to the classical garment). This was a wide piece of cloth, folded in half with a space left for the head, into a plain rectangle. It was not cut out at all, but when a girdle was added, the material was pulled in a drapery form on the arms which resembled loose sleeves. It was decorated, like the man's dalmatic, with the two bands of color or decoration called clavii. The empresses

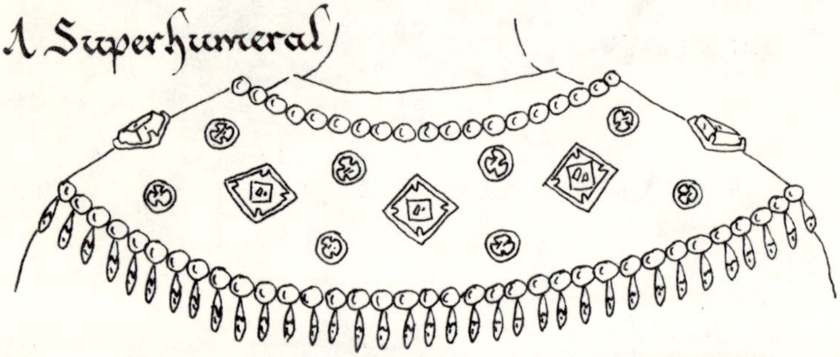

wore a second stola over this, and a length of unshaped fabric draped over all called the palla. This was folded at one end to form a panel like the man's lorum, brought over the left shoulder, unfolded, then brought around the right side under the arm, up over the left shoulder again, and allowed to fall on the ground behind. Over all this the empress wore a very wide jewelled collar with a border of drop pearls (called the superhumeral) which was to become characteristic and distinctive in Byzantine women's garb.

By the next century the palla had been largely discarded, and woman's costume had come to be almost identical in design to men's. A tunic with long, tight sleeves and a heavy border or embroidery at wrist and hem was worn, sometimes alone and sometimes with a dalmatic of the same kind as the men's. This still had the clavii, and was held at the waist by a round belt. These two garments continued to be worn throughout the entire Byzantine period. Decoration changed, of course.

A Noble Lady of the 8th century

In the eighth century, the clavii were replaced by a single wide band of decoration down the center front, expanding into a wide round band at the neck and a wide hem at the bottom. There were also two bands on the lower sleeve above the hem. The dalmatic could also be decorated like the men's with a heavily jeweled wide hem and segmentae on the shoulders and front at knee level. Sleeve hems were sometimes decorated and sometimes not. The round belt continued to be worn. During the tenth through twelfth centuries, the dalmatic was sometimes made of a diaphanous shot fabric over a foundation of heavy silk. Over this the empress wore the lorum like the emperor. In the eleventh century, the dalmatic was cut shorter, about three-quarter length in the skirt and sleeves, almost exactly like the Anglo-Saxon gwn, with a narrower border on hem and sleeves. The wide jeweled collar continued to be worn with all these styles. One unusual design, which appeared in a tenth-century textile, (representing allegorically the Byzantine Empire)

was a tunica of the usual type with over it a three-quarter length, sleeveless, sideless surcote with a V-neck and an elaborate girdle with two pendants about a foot long in front. The lady's hair was worn in two long plaits. This was not a common style, and should not be taken as typical.

Aside from this one example, the headdress worn by Byzantine women remained largely unchanged from the fourth century onward. It began as a small

Byzantine Women's Headdress

cap surrounded by a stuffed roll, described by Norris as "a skullcap surrounded by a miniature motor tyre". (Norris I, P. 169). The stuffed roll was decorated with five bands of a different color edged with pearls. Several strings of pearls were often added to hang down over the ears to shoulder level, the number depending on individual preference. This style was worn in various materials and degrees of decoration by all classes. The empress also wore, within the stuffed roll, a diadem or crown, the shape of which changed with the century. The empress alone was also allowed to wear the paludamentum; other ladies wore semicircular cloaks or other long shawls which had no ceremonial significance. Women's shoes were like men's: heelless slippers, often with a cut-out section on the top of the foot, or pedules.

Jewelry was more important to Byzantine costume than to that of most countries and periods, because it was not really an accessory but an integral part of the costume. Jewels were not yet faceted. Jewels, plaques of gold and enamel, gold wire embroidery, and especially pearls were used lavishly as trim on garb by both men and women. When this was added to a garment of cloth of gold, the effect was that of a sculptured metal figure. Mosaics and enamelling were highly developed, and many items were added to the clothing: huge, elaborate earrings several inches in length, belts made of gold plates hinged together, bracelets worn over the tight sleeves of the tunica, fibulae or clasps to hold cloaks together, rings, reliquaries, crosses, and so on. Except for the poorest classes, Byzantine garb was not complete without a lot of jewelry.

....

We will now deal briefly with some of the peripheral peoples of Europe during the Dark Ages before coming to the mainstream of Merovingian and Anglo-Saxon garb. The Russians were invaded and settled by the Scandanavian tribes, but during the tenth century came more and more under the influence of Byzantium, especially after Prince Vladimir of Kiev was converted to Orthodoxy and wed the sister of the emperor. The costume of the nobility in the Kievan Empire during this period may be described as virtually identical to Byzantine fashion, and traces of this influence persisted in native costume until modern times. The common people wore a type of tunic and pants similar to the German fashion, and this style also persisted in muzik dress down to the twentieth century.

The Huns and Avars wore a T-tunic of narrow material which formed small cap sleeves; their arms and legs were bare. Their fabric was woven from the hair of the bactrian camel, dromedary, yak, goat, or sheep, or made of a linen woven from flax. The poor wore a coarse hempen fabric made of bark, probably much like burlap. These tunics were trimmed with fur around the low, round neckline and elsewhere, or with simple embroidery. For warmth they wore a large fur-covered skin fastened around the shoulders, and on their heads a small, slightly pointed cap with a brim of fur. They also wore leggings of leather and simple leather shoes cut in one piece.

The Celts were a more artistic race with a relatively high culture, although a fierce and war-like one. They were widespread in Gaul, Britain, Ireland, and Scotland before the Roman era, but by the time of the Dark Ages were mainly confined to Ireland, Wales, Brittany, and Scotland. They also provided an influence on British costume which persisted under the Roman veneer.

Celtic cloth was made of wool and flax, and was dyed in many colors, as described in the Evolution of Fabric chapter. Cloth was often woven or sewn in horizontal stripes or checks, often in a number of different colors like a patchwork quilt. The three main elements of men's dress were the short tunic, the bracco, and cloak. The tunic, called "crys" was the same classic T-tunic we have met so often before. Sometimes long sleeves were added by piecing the openings for the arms. The crys usually reached only to thigh length. The bracco were simple trousers, cut in two pieces like pajama pants (front and back) sewed up the side and inseam, and gathered at the waist with a length of rope or cross-gartered up the leg to the knee to keep them close to the body. Again, sometimes the bracco were no more than cross-gartered leggings reaching to the knee. The shoes were simply a piece of leather with holes punched around the top and a thong was called a sagum, and was made in any shape: square, oblong, circular or semi-circular. It was fastened with a fibula or primitive pin shaped like a belt buckle or a safety pin. This was often beautifully decorated for the nobility. The sagum was made of cloth (often bright red) or occasionally a skin.

A Celt

Celtic women also liked fabric in stripes or squares of many colors. Queen Boadicea was described by Dion Cassius, a Greek writer with the Roman invasion of Britain, as wearing a tunica, full-length, of blue, red, and yellow. This tunica might be belted or loose, with long sleeves, short, or none at all. Men and women alike wore their hair long and flowing, or sometimes in braids, and women wore the same kind of sagum as the men. At times a knee-length overdress with elbow-length sleeves was worn over the tunica. These garments, like those of the man, were constructed on the lines of the simple T-tunic already described. Middle and lower-class women might wear just a long skirt to the ankle, with a skin vest laced up the center, or a Y-shaped collar which encircled the neck and then came down the center front between the breasts (left bare) in a panel to hold up the skirt.

The Irish Celts wore the same basic dress with the crys of any length from knee to ankle, and the bracco. However, they also wore a loincloth belted at the waist, called the "kelt" and the ancestor of the kilt which they carried with them into Scotland. Around the lower legs they also wore the short bracco. The sagum was often decorated with horizontal bands of checked trim or weave. Bands of Celtic knotwork were used as borders on garb, appli-que, embroideries, or woven strips. The Celts loved bright colors, and used several in one outfit: red, gold, blue, purple.

A Teutonic Woman

The Teutonic tribes included the Scandanavians, the several Goths, the Angles, Saxons, and Jutes, Lombards, Vandals, and various other northern peoples. Their basic garb has been described under the Varangian Guard: the same old short T-tunic, bracco, and cloak. For protection the warrior wore either a wide leather corselet reaching from armpit to hip and held up by suspender-like straps or a short shirt of scaled mail. Helmets with horns or wings were used, but some more modern authori-ties believe that these were purely ceremonial, and not worn into battle.

The women wore either the short-sleeved, ankle-length T-tunic or two pieces of cloth sewn together across the shoulders and held at the waist with a belt. Over this was worn an open-sided surcote or apron caught at the shoulders with two large pins, or a hip-length short-sleeved jacket, and the same sagum. The apron was often elaborately embroidered. As the different tribes migrated through Europe, they adopted the local clothing. The Ostrogoths of Theoderic in Italy, for example, were entirely Romanized in dress except for the bracco, and during their passage through the eastern areas, the Goths also adapted the persian cap and thigh-length open coat which was overlapped in front and belted closed like a car-coat.

None of these "barbarian" peoples were really barbarians in the sense that they had no arts and crafts. Indeed, it would take many pages to even begin to do justice to their excellent artifacts, but I will touch on them only briefly here, since they really require a separate article of their own. The Celtic and Germanic peoples were highly skilled in metalworking, not only for weapons, but for ornaments, fibulae, and decorations. Gold was rare, but many beautiful things were made of brightly polished iron and bronze. Fibulae and double-sided clasps used to fasten cloaks, earrings, bracelets, arm-bands, belt decorations, and "charms" or plaques were popular. The torque, or necklace open in the front, was worn by important people. Research on human sacrifices dug up from the Danish bogs indicates that this design was probably sacred to the Goddess and worn only by chiefs or those dedicated to her. Spiral design, twisted ropes, and a series of knobs set on a smooth rod were popular designs. But the true glory of this jewelry, found mainly in Frankish and Lombard pieces, were the exquisite designs of figures and interlaced design done in raised lines of metal inlaid with glass enamel or jewels, very often of a deep, glowing garnet red which seems infused with an inner fire.

....

The Merovigian Franks and the Anglo-Saxon English were closely related in origin (being various Germanic tribes which invaded during the migration period), and their dress developed from the same Germanic style of short-sleeved, thigh-length tunic and bracco with pedules. Originally (in the fifth century) they wore their hair in a strange way. It was shaved up the nape of the neck about half way, the rest of the hair was allowed to grow long, and some was caught up in a pony-tail on top of the head, while the rest hung down on either side of the face. After they settled in Gaul, this odd hairstyle changed, and the nobles wore their hair long, either loose or braided in two plaits, while the lower classes were required to wear theirs short. The Franks also wore

A Frank of the 5th century

on occasion, a fur vest or sleeveless jerkin which reached to just above the tunic hem, and sometimes went barelegged. Tatooing in spiral patterns was popular through the eighth century, covering the arms and legs completely. The common sagum was worn for warmth.

After Clovis became king of Gaul in the sixth century and was recognized as a separate ruler by the Roman emperor Anastius, the Merovingian court adopted Byzantine dress for state wear. This included the knee-length tunic with long sleeves, and the paludamentum cloak, although both were much more simply decorated. There was no tablion on the mantle, and the embroidered border did not usually have jewels. However, the Merovingians continued to wear bracco and pedules with the Byzantine-style tunic. The crown was also Byzantine in design but made locally. The common people continued to wear the Germanic tunic described previously.

Noble women of the Merovingian period also wore a style derived from Byzantium: the long tunica, dalmatica with full sleeves and clavii, and a belt. But the Merovingian ladies did not wea the heavy collar, or the Byzantine headdress. Instead, they wore a veil held in place with a long pin on top of the head. The common women wore the Germanic style described under Teutons sometimes with Roman influences depending on the individual.

At the end of the eighth century the Merovingians were replaced by the Carolingians, the dynasty of Charlemagne. For every day, the chroniclers recorded, the king wore the dress of the people. Thi was a linen undertunic, knee-length, cross-gartered linen bracco, pedules, and an overtunic slightly shorter than the undertunic, with decorative border at the hem, wrist, and upper arm. There was a belt and overall a circular cloak. On his head was a cap rather like a Scots bonnet. For state dress, the emperor wore the same garb as the Byzantine emperor, including the elaborately decorated paludamentum and the lorum decorated with jewels. Later kings of the tenth and eleventh centuries abandoned these last two items and wore only an ankle-length full robe of soft fabric and a girdle with a long tongue hanging down in front past knee level. The overtunic, however, continued to be made of Byzantine fabric and embroidered in that style with borders and segmentae.

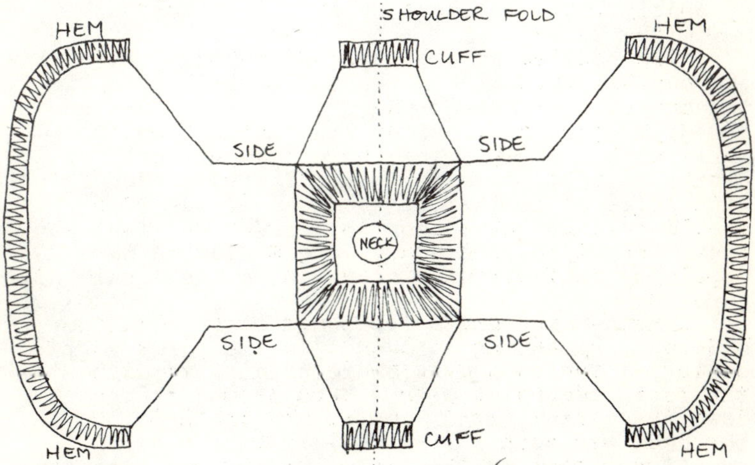

Cut of a Saxon Tunic

The Anglo-Saxons in England wore garb of the same design: the short, long-sleeved tunic decorated with borders at wrist, hem, and upper arm. From the tenth century, however, the tunic had a new shape. It was still made in the T-tunic fashion out of one piece of fabric, but now the skirt was cut so that it flared abruptly at the waist level to make a fuller skirt. An invisible belt pulled the waist in allowing a little of the cloth to drape over it, and making the skirt fall in graceful zig-zag folds. There were variations on this style. Occasionally, especially among the Germans of the eleventh century, the bottom of the tunic was cut square across instead of rounded at the sides, so that a long point fell down at each side of the skirt. (If you cut a skirt in a triangle shape with sharp corners at the bottom, you will see how this happens). The neck might be a round hole or have a slit down the front. Sometimes among the lower classes, for hard physical work, the tunic hem was caught up in the belt above each thigh to create an effect not unlike a droopy diaper. Leg coverings included knee-length or (rarely) full-length bracco, socca or loose leggings, sometimes caught up in the back and drooping loosely in front, or, most often, hosa and pedules. The hosen were eithe with or without the foot part and were attached (probably laced to short bracco (like shorts)beneath the tunic.

The pedules were of various styles: made like bedroon slippers with a V-shape on each side of the ankle, buttoned up the front, or cut out on the upper part of the foot and fastened on the ankle with a strap. They were made of leather, cloth, or felt, sometimes embroidered or decorated, with soles of leather or wood. Hair was worn shoulder-length or longer in a round cut like the Byzantine style, and beards and mustaches were popular. Semi-circular cloaks were the usual outer garment.

Anglo-Saxon dress for women began with considerable Byzantine influence in the early eighth century a tunica and dalmatic hanging straight to the feet, decorated with a band around the neck, down the center front, and around the hem. On the head was worn a long veil without a circlet, reaching almost to the feet. By the ninth century, the distinctive Saxon style had emerged. This consisted of an undertunic with close sleeves and an

Saxon

overtunic with wide sleeves, sometimes to the wrist but often only to the elbow. This overtunic might be full-length or three-quarter length; if it was full-length it was usually held up on each side or in front so as to appear shorter and to show the undertunic. This created a graceful drapery which was very much admired. The neck was round, with or without a slit in front, but it was usually hidden by the veil. This veil was either a large rectangle which was centered on the head and had one end wrapped around the throat and tossed over the shoulder, or it was an oval with a circle cut toward the front which fitted over the face. The veil was held in place with a circlet or crown.

The overtunic was known as the gwn, gyn, or gunna, and was decorated with either an all-over pattern (usually of Byzantine inspiration, such as large circles) or bands of embroidery at wrist and hem, with or without a center strip. The gunna was cut in the same way as the man's T-tunic, but it widened much less abruptly in the skirt, which was a gently triangular line from about the waist to the hem. It might be only ankle-length, or it might be longer in back to form a short train, and it might or might not have a girdle. With it, the ordinary semi-circular cloak might be worn, but there was also a style similar to the design of the veil, which had a round opening about one third of the way back and was one solid piece, so that it formed a short capelet in the front, reaching about to the waist, and fell down much further in back.

A Noble Woman of the 9-11 th centuries

BIBLIOGRAPHY

In addition to the volumes cited in the previous chapter, the following works were consulted for this section:

Ashe, Geoffery. The Quest for Arthur's Britain, Frederick A. Praeger, New York, 1968.

Encyclopedia Britannica.

Houston, May. Ancient Greek, Roman, and Byzantine Costume and Decoration, Adam and Charles Black, London, 1966.

Payne, Blanche. History of Costume, Harper and Row, New York, 1965.

Rice, David Talbot, ed. The Dawn of European Civilization, McGraw-Hill, New York, 1965.

Wood Carving from 13th Cent.
St. Louis and his wife Margaret

Costume of the 12th & 13th c.

From this point on, I will be giving the chronology of dress mainly in terms of England, with which I am most familiar and which has had the most written about it. Costume was fairly homogeneous in Western Europe through the later medieval period, for no major national styles had yet developed. Indeed, until at least the late fifteenth and sixteenth centuries, there was virtually no sense of national identity as we think of it, and even then, except among the highest nobility who tended to identify the nation with themselves, any identification in between membership in the local fief and in the universal family of Christianity was shaky. England was something of an exception. Because it was an island, and because in legal theory it was all one great fief under the king, rather than a collection of great dutchies like France or Spain, it had more of a sense of nationhood. But the intense patriotism that Shakepeare puts in the mouth of Henry V, for example, is largely an anachronism.

Fashion tended to evolve in the western areas of Europe (England, France, Italy, Burgundy, Provance) and migrate slowly eastward, although this was not universal. Hense, while fashionable folk in Burgundy were wearing the steeple henin and V-necked gown in the fifteenth century, the aristocracy of Bohemia was still dressed in the cotehardies of the mid-Fourteenth century. Along with poor communications, another conservative influence was the tendency to pass clothing down from one generation to another. Cloth was expensive, sewing and embroidery were time-consuming, and many styles were not fitted closely to the body, so garb was worn until it fell apart. The styles of one era continued to be seen for years thereafter. Again, except among the highest classes, few people could afford to make new clothes very often, and when new ones did appear, many simple people might not even realize that a change had taken place at court. Peasant clothing, in particular, might be a hundred years behind the fashion among the king's household. In general, this caused little inconvenience, for fashion changed so slowly that it was hardly noticeable in a single person's lifetime, which was probably no more than thirty-five or forty years in most cases.

With the coming of the Normans, English fashion naturally was changed. (State royal dress did remain the same for several centuries yet, based as before on the Byzantine tunic and wide-sleeved dalmatic). Next to the skin was worn the sherte of chainsil (fine white linen). This was just what it sounds like: a shirt, cut on the T-tunic principle, as all these garments continued to be, falling straight to the knee and slit at the sides, with fairly tight, straight sleeves. It was some-

Two 12th century Borders

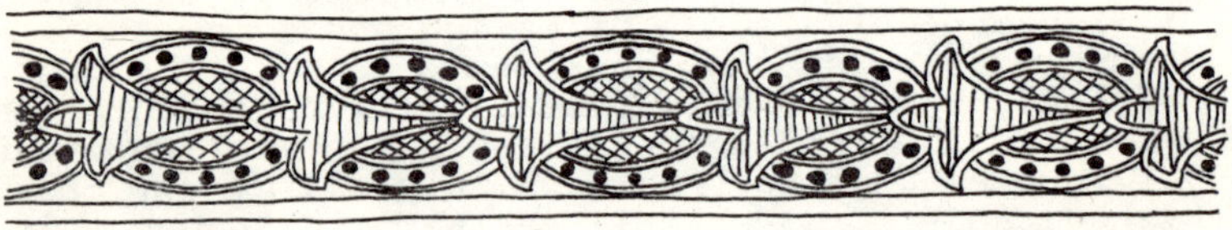

times embroidered with a border at the round neck and wrists. Borders were usually geometric designs such as circles, triangles, or interlaced lines, or in the shape of simple, repetitious natural forms. Occasionally, an overgarment might have an all-over pattern composed of separate motifs sprinkled over the garb like a pattern of polka-dots.

Over the sherte the jube could be added for warmth or luxury. This was of the same design as the sherte, but had sleeves only to the elbow. One or two overtunics would be added next, and finally an overtunic of a fancier fabric on top. Each layer might be slightly shorter than the one below, so that all the garments were visible. Strong colors were favored, often ones we would consider to clash when used together, and the effect was often striking. The tunic might be worn at knee length, when it was called a cotte, but for formal dress and among the upper classes, it was more often worn ankle-length or longer. This was called the robe or surcote. The sleeves of the robe were close

Shape of the Cotte

at the wrist or moderately wide, say about a foot or eighteen inches around. The cut of the tunic was similar to the previous fashion but had two new features: the skirt flared much less strongly and the sleeves were now added at an angle sloping down from the shoulder. The lower sleeve would be sewn on about six inches down, and this seam was often covered by a band of embroidery. Hosen were worn on the legs, but these were quite baggy, like heavy tights a size too large. Shoes were flat, heel-less slippers with pointed toes. They might be high around the ankle with an opening on each side, like victorian elastic boots without the elastic, cut on top and held around the ankle with a strap, or open like a slipper with a higher section behind the heel. During the reign of Henry I (ca. 1100) there was a brief fashion of elongating the toe greatly, stiffening it with a stuffing, and curving it up sharply in a curl or shape like a fish's tail.

Two interesting short-lived fashions appeared during the century following the Norman conquest. They were influenced by the fact that much of the fabric used by the upper class at this time was soft and thin, and draped in small folds. The first of these styles occurred during the reign of Henry I (1100-1135), when it became fashionable to elongate greatly all the outer garments. Skirts were so

A Fish Tailed Shoe

long and full they had to be tucked up into the girdle to permit walking, mantles trailed on the ground, and sleeves hung down a foot over the edge of the hand. Beards and hair were also worn as long as possible. The other style, brought back from the east, was worn between 1130 and 1150. This was an elaborate, high-fashion garment known as the <u>bliaut</u>. It was worn over an undertunic of the usual type, floor-length with close sleeves. The top was shaped like an ordinary tunic, fitting rather closely to the body and with moderately open long sleeves; the neck was an open V-shape of the kind found on many contemporary tunics. At the waist

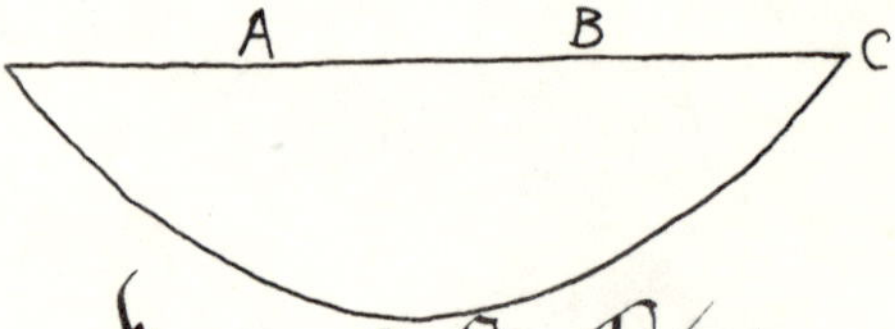

Cut of the Skirt

The Bliaut

a skirt was added, cut in two pieces shaped like rounded triangles. They were gathered and sewn to the top in a section in the center (A and B in the diagram), then left to fall free along the section B and C at the sides. The bliaut was evidently fastened down the back to hold it close to the body, while the skirt thus formed interesting triangular folds of uneven length. Various other minor articles of dress were brought back after the crusades at this time. Overtunics of Byzantine cut and decoration, the eastern type of cloak, and the habit of wearing a deep band of embroidery (or more probably a separate collar) around the neckline, sometimes set with jewels.

Neither of these extreme styles were popular with the ordinary people or endured for long. The average man of high rank wore an ankle-length undertunic and a slightly shorter one over it with close or slightly wide sleeves and a heavy band of embroidery (if the fabric was heavy enough to bear the weight) at neck, wrist, and hem. The lower class used the same basic costume cut to knee length.

A new garment appeared at this time, one which was to have a long and complex history: the hood. The first hood was cut like a trianglar funnel or dunce-cap with a hole near the top end for the head. The point hung to the back of the head, and the longer base end formed a cape on the shoulders.

The hood might also be added to a cape. At the time of the invasion, the Normans wore their hair in a short, round cut, sometimes shaved up the nape of the neck to the level of the ears (mainly a military cut) or cut off at the base of the head. They were clean-shaven, but at times wore long mustaches like the villian in a victorian mellodrama. After the Conquest, however, they went to an extreme in the opposite direction and developed very long hair falling far down the back, and beards, often forked, almost to the waist. This went along with the elongated style of garb mentioned above.

The most immediately visible difference in women's dress after the conquest was that the three-quarters length gunna was replaced by a full-length overgown fitted more closely to the body. This garment was cut in the same way as the man's tunic, with the same sloping sleeves and line of embroidery on the upper arm. The neck was cut round with a slit in front, decorated all around with a band of embroidery, as were the wrists and hem. Around the waist was a single girdle with a long tongue hanging down past knee length in front. These girdles were often decorated with bands of metal, inset jewels, gold beads and tassels or metal end pieces. On the head was a long veil held in place with a circlet. This was undoubtedly one of the most graceful and

Norman Noble Lady

elegant costumes ever worn, with a classic beauty of pure line. The undergarment worn with this was the camise or chemise, our old friend the smock, made of very fine, soft fabric such as silk, shinsil, or fine wool. This was sewn together in an interesting way which can be seen in an illustration better than it can be described in words. The neckband and the ends of the sleeves were composed of several rows of small cords covered with the material of the smock. The shoulder was gathered into this neckband, and the stitched down with a row or two of the same cording at the top of the arm, and the sleeve was gauffered at the forearm to keep it close to the arm. The front section of the chemise was added at right angles to the yoke formed by this treatment of the arm. The neckband was closed by a button and loop, and was often decorated with embroidery in gold or color, since it was frequently seen above the neck o of the overgown.

Two new ideas came into being during this period: lacing, and what inevitably followed it, the corset.

The Chemise

Plaiting Hair

As fashion began to favor gowns fitting closely to the figure, ladies put in a panel at the back or (occasionally) under the arm which could be laced together to fit the garment tightly to the body from bust to hips. Small waists were celebrated in love poetry, not for the first or last time, and to achieve them ladies put on the <u>corse</u>. This was a garment of about the shape and size of a long-line bra, which began just below the breasts and ended at the line of the hip bone. It was stiffened with thin strips of wood or metal set into the material, which was fabric or leather. It was held on the shoulder with thin straps and laced tightly up the front. All medieval and Renaissance corsets followed this basic pattern, for, for unknown reasons, the dressmakers of this period never seemed to master the construction of bra cups for the breasts (or perhaps never felt they were necessary). Like most innovations designed to increase feminine attractiveness, the corse was regarded with suspicion by the clergy, who claimed that it encouraged letchery. An illuminated manuscript of the period survives in the British Museum, showing the Devil clad in a tight-laced corset.

While the basic line of the Norman gown remained the same, a number of different kinds of sleeves were added. During the reign of Henry I, women also participated in the fad for very long garments, wearing vast trains, long veils, and voluminous triangular sleeves with the open base at the wrist, sometimes tied in knots to prevent them dragging on the ground. Other designs used with the more conservative gown were: shorter triangular shapes reaching about to the thigh, slightly open sleeves like those of the men, a gard-corps type which had a hole about half way down the front for the hand to emerge and then

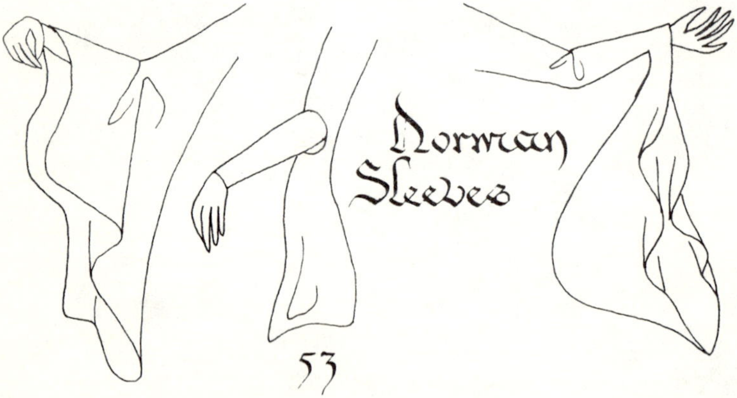

fell in a widening bell shape several feet further and the <u>maunch</u> style. This last fitted close on the arm to just above the wrist, then opened up into a narrow pendant falling about a yard from the wrist and ending in a slightly curved bottom line. This sleeve became a heraldic charge.

The semi-circular mantle was still in fashion for both men and women. It was now often fastened by sewing a ring to one corner of the front, bringing the other top corner through it and knotting it, or by attaching a rich cord to each side of the neck-hole leaving the center open down the front of the costume. When the full veil and wimple were worn, ladies dressed their hair in a bun at the base of the neck, but when the open veil was worn alone, two long braids were fashionable, the longer the better. Each braid was divided into two (not three) plaits which were bound together with a ribbon passing first around one plait, then around both, then around the other plait, then around both again, and so forth. The lower section of each braid might be encased in a tube of silk or other fabric and decorated with two ribbons criss-crossed up and down the braid. This casing ended in a tassel or metal ornament to hold the braid straight. If the lady's own hair was deficient, the cases would be stuffed with same substance to make the braids seen longer than they were; they were supposed to reach to the knee or lower. The method of braiding the hair may be seen in the illustration showing the chemise.

During the short period that the male bliaut was in fashion, the ladies had a version of their own called by the same name. Compared with the styles which preceeded and followed it, this was a fussy and unattractive costume, and it is not surprising that it lasted only about twenty years. Over the chemise the lady put on a long fairly full gown of thin, soft fabric, rather like a very light-weight gauze. The full width back and front was gathered on the shoulders into innumerable tiny pleats. These may have been set with a hot iron or pressure, perhaps by broomstick pleating like the skirt of an old fashioned squaw dress. The pleats were sewn down just below the neckline across the entire garment at about the level of the underarm. The sleeves were treated in the same way: they were cut on the cross of the fabric, very full, in a wide triangular shape reaching almost to the feet, then pleated into the armhole and stitched down a few inches further down the arm. The bliaut is the first medieval example of a garment with set-in sleeves, but this method of construction did not become general until the next century. Over this dress there was a wide belt or corselet. The belt was of plain soft but sturdy fabric fastened around the body tightly from under the bust to the hips. The corselet or corsage was a sleeveless short overtunic, laced tightly up the back (?) and also reaching to about the hips. In the illuminations this garment has a waffle-like diamond pattern overall, and this has been variously interpreted as some sort of knit or elastic material, quilting, or decorative stitching added to strengthen or adorn the corsage, running diagonally both directions to form a criss-cross design. Sometimes jewels were set at each intersection of the lines. Over the corsage was added the double girdle, which was worn only with this style and not with the Norman gown. This girdle was a richly decorated flat belt which was brought around the front just under the bustline, crossed in back, and brought around again in a curve that exactly followed the lower edge of the corsage. The two ends were finished with long cords which were tied together in front then allowed to fall down the skirt. The corselet was caught at the neck with a broach. The hair was dressed as before described in long braids, a veil, and a circlet.

Woman's Bliant

During the last half of the twelfth century, both men and women returned to loose-fitting simple tunics, long or short. The cut was considerably looser on the upper body, although the construction continued to be on the T-tunic pattern with a slit at the neck as before. A few minor innovations appeared at this time, among them the first restrained examples of <u>dagging</u> and <u>parti-color</u>, which would be more characteristic of the fourteenth century and will be discussed there. Gloves with separate fingers instead of mittens were first created at this time. They were first extremely expensive, decorated with gold and jewels on the back of the hand, and were available to the highest nobility only. Gloves continued to be worn through the rest of the period, and an elaborate set of customs evolved about the way they were handled. Rings were often worn on the outside of the glove, a fashion which persisted until Elizabethan times.

Two or more tunics, each slightly shorter than the one below, were common, and bright colors continued to be usual. For example, a manuscript from 1121-1148 (the St. Eadmunsbury Bible) shows a figure in tunics of bright blue and grass green, a scarlet cloak, magenta hosen, and electric blue boots! For riding or general free movement the tunic might be slit up the front and back, or on the sides to about the level of the crotch. Hoods were now cut in a new shape, fitting more closely around the neck. The head part and the cape might be cut separately or on one piece. A hat was often worn

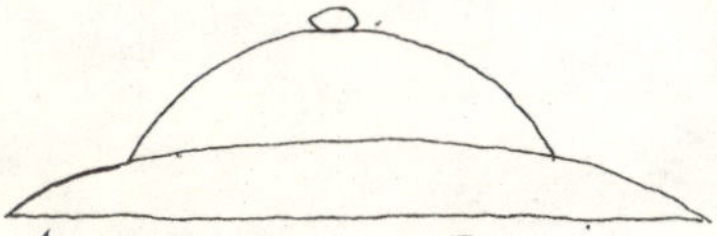

Dish Cober Hat

Hoods

over the hood, or the hood might be thrown back and the hat worn on the bare head. One popular hat was small, composed of a shallow brim and a plain, low, rounded crown. The brim might be made of fur, or it might be rather flat. There was often a short point or a knob on top, in which case the whole thing looked remarkably like a dish-cover from an elaborate room-service set. Hair was cut short at about ear level, and curled all over the head.

Late 12th century

Ladies also returned to the earlier style of a straight long tunic which was loose and unfitted throughout and held at the waist by a long single girdle. A new accessory added to the veil and circlet in place of the wimple was the barbette or chinstrap, made popular by Eleanor of Aquitaine. It was a simple strip of white linen, narrow at the chin and widening toward the ends, which were crossed on top of the head under the veil and pinned in place. The wimple was used as well, for the barbette was no more than a miniature or vestigal version of the wimple itself, which was also called the barbe. Both were used to hold the hair in place; the braids, now without artificial additions were crossed in back, wound around the head in a coronet, and pinned or tucked in on top in front.

Ladies' garments continued to be cut on the old T-tunic pattern with the V-neck, sometimes open and sometimes narrow, but gores were now added, if desired, for greater width in the skirt.

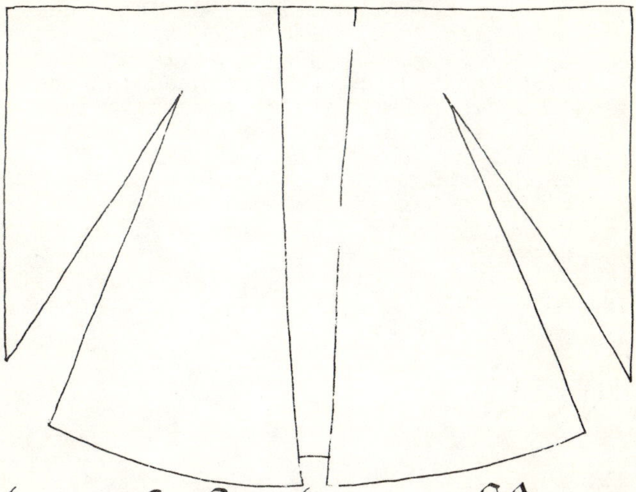

Cut of the Oriental Surcote

A new overgarment, or a revival of an old one, came into use near the end of the century. Its first version appeared at the period when the bliaut was popular, some years earlier, and also had its origins in a garment brought back from the east: the oriental surcote. This was a loose overgarment, open in a wide V all the way down the front and held at the waist by a clasp. It reached to about the knees, and was cut like the little girls' dresses known as "angel dresses" as shown in the illustration above. When it arrived in England, it was made of some very light fabric, often transparent gauze, edged with a band of heavy trim to hold it down. It made a pretty addition to the delicate fabric of the bliaut. Later, however, when the under garment became heavier, this garment was modified.

The front was made closed and the sleeves were shortened to the elbow, while the body of the gown was cut narrower, so that the final result looked exactly like the Saxon gunna. This dress was now worn for warmth, so it was lined with fur and, logically, called the pelice or pelicon (pelice being Norman French for "fur"). Any garment lined with fur might thus be properly called a pelicon, and the name was applied to a variety of different overgarments which will be noted in later pages.

The thirteenth century was the apex of feudalism, the most fully "medieval" of centuries; it was also one of the most simple in style of garb. Great stress was placed upon the richness of the fabric used, but there was almost no decorative trim or fanciful elaboration. For fabric of the period, see the first chapter The Evolution of Fabric. The basic garment continued to be the loose long tunic before described. A new overgarment which was to have a long history came into popularity in the first third of the century: the cyclas, also called ciclatoun, syglaton, sideless surcote, and no doubt other names as well. It was created, it is said, for the

The Cyclas

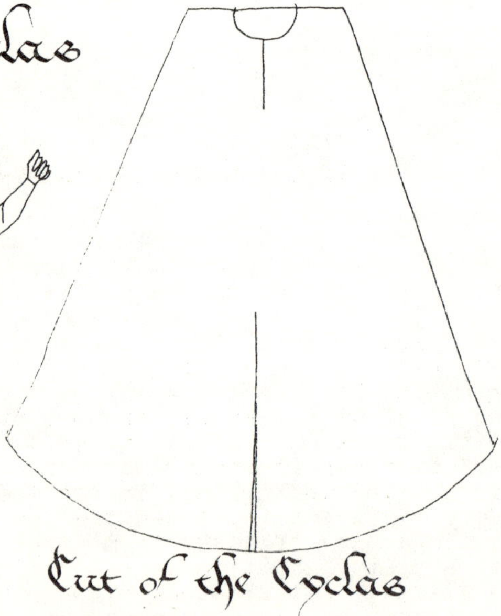

Cut of the Cyclas

crusaders to wear in the heat of the Holy Land over their armor to keep it from burning them. It was a slightly flared triangular T-tunic of the usual sort, but without sleeves, often slit up the front and back for riding. At first it was just a wide band of fabric with a hole for the head, open completely up both sides and held in place with a long-tongued single girdle. It might be any length from mid-shin level to floor-length, but during this century men's clothes of any kind were never as high as the knee except among the peasant and artisan class. (These two groups were still seen in the old Saxon cotte on occasion). About mid-century, the cyclas began to be buttoned or sewn part-way up the sides from armhole to knee. Later a variety of interesting sleeves were added to the cyclas, and from this point on sleeves were usually added separately in the modern way rather than cut with the body of the garb as before.

When it had sleeves, the cyclas was known as the gard-corps. The most typical gardcorps sleeve was a wide rectangle, open at the bottom end and falling to knee level. The other end was set in a line of vertical pleats or tucks, and an opening was left in the front for the arm to pass out of the sleeve at shoulder level. This style of gardcorps was also worn by ladies only while riding horseback. Other sleeves which might be added included an open panel that fell behind the arm from shoulder level, wide sleeves like the dalmatic, and simple slits like a caftan, or plain sleeves with a shoulder opening for the arm like those first described but without the pleats. Occasionally, a low standing collar might be added around the wide round neckline. A long-tongued girdle might be added, but the the closed gardcorps or surcote it was more common to leave the garb to fall freely in graceful folds. Moving toward the later dagging fashion, the cyclas's hem and sides were often cut out in patterns, usually the heraldic dividing and border lines such as nebulee, engrailed, embattled, dancette and so on. When this was done the garment was called a <u>cointise</u> (meaning "fanciful").

Another sort of surcote was called the <u>ganache</u>. This was cut like a T-tunic in one piece with wide but short sleeves and a voluminous hood. It might be sewn shut or left open down both sides; it was often lined with fur.

Bardcorp

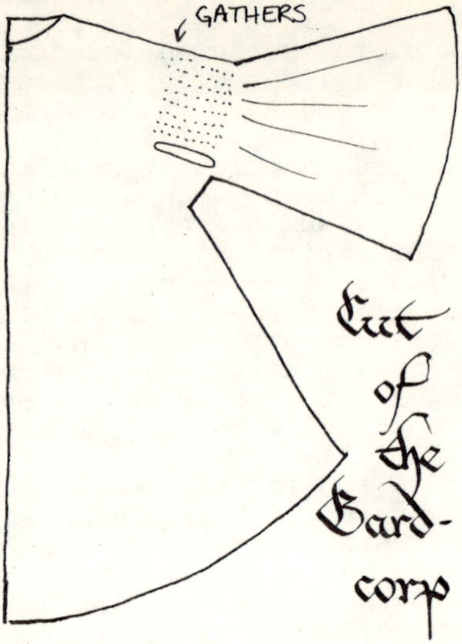

Cut of the Bard-corp

Besides the dish-cover hat mentioned before, men also wore the hood, now with the point on top elongated down as far as the waist or below and called the liripipe, and the coif. This last was the most characteristic headcovering of the thirteenth century. It was white, shaped just like a baby-bonnet, and was worn day and night, indoors or out, and even under hoods or other hats. Hair was cut short at about chin level and rolled up in a curl all around the bottom. Toward 1225, the hair was parted just above the forehead and the short fringe thus formed was curled forward in one long curl across the forehead.

The Coif

Shoes continued to be short ankle-length boots of the sort illustrated in the section on fabric as an example of thirteenth century pattern. Mantles were of the same semi-circular type, and were held in a variety of ways by men and women: by a band across the chest, clasped on one shoulder, draped like a shawl, over one shoulder and drawn around under the other arm, and so on.

The ladies of the thirteenth century wore a gown of exactly the same cut as the man's tunic, but reaching to the floor, and if this were worn alone it would be confined at the waist by the same long-tongued girdle. The corse continued to be worn as well, although the line of the dress no longer required it. The front of the gown might be left open to the waist if an under-gown was worn. Women took to the cyclas shortly after the men, but often wore it long and trailing both front and back. It was sometimes worn

A Cyclas Sewn-up

without the girdle even when it was open on the sides. When the cyclas was sewn up, it fitted fairly close to the waist, then had wide gores let into the skirt to create a very full, flowing train. Whatever the overdress, it would be full, trained, ungirdled, and totally undecorated, with moderately wide elbow length sleeves.

The undergown had close sleeves to the wrist. Patterned fabric was popular in stripes, small all-over geometric designs, or Byzantine patterns of brocade. Decorative borders were rare, and when used were generally scrolled designs in plant tendrils and leaves.

A number of headdresses went along with these simple gowns. At the beginning of the century, when the veil was popular, the hair might be parted across the center of the head, the front part curled on the forehead and the back braided and wrapped around the head like a coronet. Girls and young women might wear their hair flowing loose on the shoulders, plaited with a ribbon into one braid in back, or crowned with a chaplet of fresh or imitation flowers. However, it is well to remember that in this period when girls were married at twelve or fourteen, one was middle aged by twenty-five. Toward the end of the century, the two braids were curled up in a spiral on each side of the head over the ears. This was called the "ramshorn", and the tips of the braids were often left stickling out the center of the spiral to make the effect more realistic. Later the braids were covered with casings of silk before being wound into the spiral. The braids might be wound low at the sides of the head, or the hair held in place by the crispine, or net. It might be made of gold or silver cord and decorated with a jewel sewn at each intersection of the net. With the ramshorn the wimple could be worn alone, pinned to the top of the braids on each side; this was known as the gorget. A shoulder-length veil could be added, and over both veil and wimple, one of the little dish-cover hats. With the barbette, however, ladies wore a small pillbox hat made with a stiff upright brim (which could be fluted around the top) and filled in with a flat circular section. This cap was gradually widened on the sides until it formed an oval rather than a circle. The oval cap might be worn without the barbette with a short veil over the top of it. This little hat was always white. It can easily be reproduced by covering with a white fabric the stiff open circle form for bridesmaid's headdresses at fabric stores, and filling in the center with a stiff piece of something flat, say cardboard. The intended effect of all headdresses during this period was width, all concentrated on extending the hair or veil toward the sides.

Women's shoes were the same as men's. The mantle was very important during the thirteenth century. It was frequently made of rich fabric lined with fur, silk, or some other expensive cloth. If one of the elaborate brocades was used, a seam would be sewn up the center back and the design reversed on each side. The mantle was made long and trailing in an oval shape, with the front edge cut straight across on in a triangular shape which made the whole almost circular. Mantles were marks of respect restricted to noble lords and ladies, and an elaborate etiquette grew up surrounding wearing and displaying them.

With the development of heraldry, which came into its own in the thirteenth century, livery became popular. Members of noble households or guilds began to wear garb, of the same sort as everyday fashion, but sewn in the colors of their lord's or group's coat of arms. This was usually parti-color with the two main colors of the field and charge(s), and often decorated with a badge on the sleeve.

BIBLIOGRAPHY

In addition to the references previously mentioned, the following were used for this chapter.

C. Willett Cunnington and Phyllis Cunnington, Handbook of English Medieval Costume, Boston, Plays, Inc., 1969.

Mistress of Arts Handbook of the Middle Kingdom.

Layton, Jean, trans. Medieval Costume, Armour and Weapons, London, Paul Hamlyn Ltd., 1958

After the Garden of Paradise

c. 1410

The Wonderful 14th century

It may seem strange to call the age of the Black Plague, the Peasants' Revolt and the Hundred Years' War "wonderful". But after the bland gard of the thirteenth century, the fourteenth bolssomed out in vivacious styles marked by inventive fancy, wild variety, and general sartorial <u>chutspah</u>. The reason, I believe, why this change came about is discussed in the article in this volume titled "Sex and the Single Surcote".

These changes did not become significant until the social upheavals of the mid-century had been felt. At the beginning of the century circular clokes replaced semi-circular ones in fashion. These might be with or without a hood, and might be pulled on over the head or have an opening all the way up the front and slits at each side for the arms and ornamental fastenings. This was first worn in the normal way, but later the right arm was passed through the usual opening (B on the diagram) and the head through the left arm opening (Con the diagram) so that the normal head opening was now on the right shoulder. This porduced a rather strange, lopsided effect. The other novelty of this period was the introduction of the <u>chaperon</u>. The caped hood had already been elaborated by addition of a long liripipe or pointed end, which was elongated to a strip hanging up to six feet down the back of the head. Sometimes, two points were added instead of one, much shorter, from which were derived the "asses ears" of the traditional fool's cap.

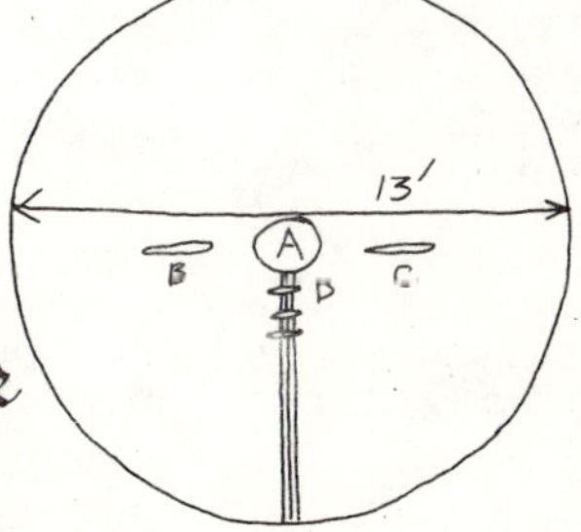

Circular Cloke Diagram

The newest innovation was to place the face opening of the hood on top of the head, wrap the liripipe around the forehead, and drape the cape part of the hood to the side or the front to form the "cockscomb". This style continued through the century. Otherwise, the simple, plain robes of the thirteenth century continued to be worn.

Women also continued to wear long, full gowns falling straight to the feet without a girdle. The sleeves of the overdress might be fairly close, absent entirely, or hanging down behind the elbow in a short, fairly narrow strip. At this time the sideless surcote was frequently laced loosely down the sides with decorative cords. The arm-hole would be cut rectangular or oval at the bottom with the width of the front panel reduced somewhat but not very much. The neckline was low and oval, so that the straps over the shoulder were not very wide. This first version was loose and rather shapeless, showing very little of the underdress, and was virtually identical to the old cyclas in construction. But it proved tenacious; with variations which will be detailed below, the sideless gown continued as a ceremonial garment down to the Tudor period.

As mentioned previously, the <u>pelicon</u> came to be any garment lined with fur. One type which was popular at this time was the circular cloke mentioned above, worn in the normal fashion with side slits for the arms and a small shoulder cape attached. The shoulder cape was slit to the neckline, and the sides falling over the shoulders were often turned up to the neck, so that the cape seemed to come to a point in the front and back. There was still little use made of trim on garments, but when it was found, it was usually a scrolling pattern of leaves and flowers in a fairly naturalistic style.

Hair was dressed on the sides of the face, as it had been in the previous century. It was plaited in two braids, wound in circles at each side, and often worn with a full wimple pinned to the top of the braids at each side. Over this might be worn a short veil, reaching to about chin level in front and to the base of the neck in back. A flat, oval piece of goldsmith's work, with a rigid edge and a wide, thick mesh in the center might be placed on top of the head, and the veil worn over this. The effect of this hat was that of a metalic oval pancake filled with heavy chickenwire. A detail worth noting is that when the wimple was worn so that the bottom edge fell outside the neck of the gown, it was known as the guimpe.

The Chaperon

About the middle of the century a novel style appeared for both men and women: the cotehardie. This was the first garment, other than the Norman gown, which was fitted to the figure and the first formal man's garment since the early Dark Ages which showed the leg. As a result, hosen improved in cut and construction, and a shapely male limb in smooth, well-fitting hose became a major mark of masculine beauty. We are lucky enough to have a number of garments from this period which were excavated at Herjolfsness in southern Greenland, so that we can see the exact cut of the hosen and cotehardie. Herjolfsnes was a Danish colony, and presumably was reasonably familiar with the development of fashion in the rest of northern Europe, although it was certainly not a center of style. The excavation was carried out in 1921.

The Early Sideless Surcote

Among the garments found at Herjolfsnes was a pair of hosen. Heavy winter-weight tights or wrestlers' tights are usually quite adequate for Society wear. However, for those who wish to reproduce period hosen accurately, a diagram of the kind found is presented on a later page. Norris describes the method of construction as follows:

"The sides BF and DG were joined up the back of the leg, starting at the heel. As BF was longer than DG, the corner B could not coincide with C, but was drawn up above it and joined to CA, finishing at D. The triangle E was joined to the sole J. The point A was attached to the waist belt at the side of the front. This pattern is given because of its interest. It is not one recommended for good fit but illustrates a useful garment such as was worn by ordinary people".

Since the style illustrated was not very well-fitting, the upper classes wore a style cut more along the lines of another illustration, which is quite close to modern tights. However, the legs were always separate, not sewn together into one garment. They were cut on the cross of the fabric so they would stretch to fit closely and move with the wearer. There was an opening about eight inches long on the inside of the ankle, so that the hose could be drawn up over the foot, and this opening was sewn shut at each wearing of the hosen. The outside seams ABC and DEF are joined and the inside HI and RQ, with the rest of that seam left open. The gusset O joins the front and back on the inside of the ankle. N and M are sewn to the heel, and the sole joined to the instep FKJ. SA and DG are the half waist-line and the dotted areas may be added to overlap in front and back.

Early 14th cent. head-dress

With this new style, a new type of underwear was necessary. The sherte was worn with short braes called slops, cut like a pair of man's swim trunks or ladies' bikini briefs. Over these was worn the <u>paltock</u>, a waist-length tight vest laced up the front. Sleeves were always attached to the paltock, either sewn directly to the body of the garment, or laced at the arm-hole with "poynts". The hosen in turn were laced to the bottom of the paltock with <u>herlots</u> or laces (like shoe laces); this was called "trussing the poynts". After the middle of the century, the paltock was stuffed between the inner lining and the outer layer and quilted, in order to

Cut of the Herjolfsnes hosen

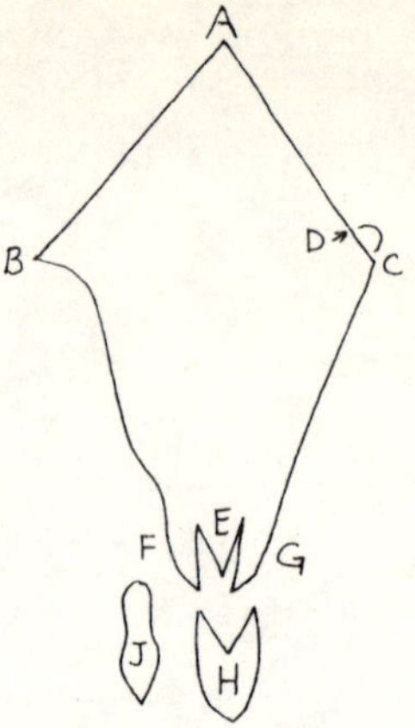

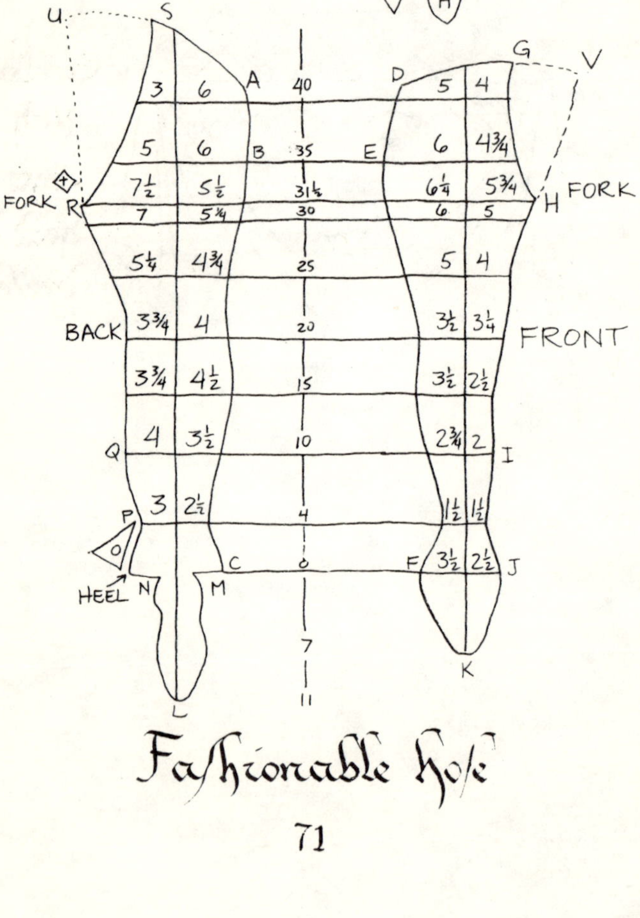

Fashionable hose

give a pigeon-chested look, and it was then known as the pourpoint. Decorative garters might also be worn below the knee. Women continued to wear short hose which reached to about the knee and were tied or gartered at the top. Naturally, however, the improved style in man's hose was carried over into women's as well.

The man's cotehardie consisted of a very tight-fitting short tunic cut in four pieces and shaped closely to the body over the pourpoint. The padded chest accentuated a slim waist and small hips, and the most fashionable male cotehardie could really only be worn by the young, slender man. It had long, tight sleeves, buttoned to the elbow, and was generally no longer than mid-thigh. Buttons were commonly added all the way from neck to hem, down the front. Tippits were sometimes added: long, narrow strips of white cloth fastened around the arm just above the elbow and falling down almost to the ground like a streamer. Around the hips, a few inches above the hem, was fastened a heavy metal belt of plaques which were generally square and often decorated with jewels, raised designs filigree, or enamel.

These belts might be in very high relief, an inch or more thick. They were fastened in front by a pin passing through slots behind the central medalion. With the cotehardie a hood was often worn, and frequently, over the hood, a small hat. A common sort of hat was made of beaver fur, with a skull cap and a narrow round rolled brim. Other styles included a floppy tricorn style turned up on the front and back, a small bagcap with a rigid brim, and a plain, round rigid shape like a railway-engine wheel.

The two most popular decorative motifs during the later fourteenth century were parti-coloring and dagging. Parti-coloring was dividing the garment down the center front and back; parti-quarterly was making each of the four pieces a different color so that the panels alternated around the figure vertically (for example) white, green, white, green. Each half, front and back, might also be divided quarterly into four squares like a giant checker board, into wide diagonal stripes, and so on. Often one of the fabrics was patterned and one plain, or both might be patterned in reverse (I.e. one white on black and the other black on white). Sleeves might continue the color of the body part or reverse it, and hosen were reversed from the color of the body part above. Dagging had been used before, as mentioned above, but reached its high point at this time. Any available edge might be cut out in shapes, often quite elaborate designs like leaves and fern fronds. Favorite places for dagges were the hem of the cotehardie, the cape of the hood, the edge of the cloak, and occasionally the ends of the sleeves if they were long and open like tippits.

The cotehardie was the first major fashion which was not cut on the T-tunic pattern. The basic shape is shown on pg. 74. An ordinary round necked shirt pattern can easily be adapted by adding several inches to the hem, fitting the waist and hip area closely, and expanding the chest area slightly if you wish to pad it. The cotehardie was usually fastened down the entire front from neck to hem by decorative loops and buttons, which were usually small balls or half-spheres. Sleeves were tight and usually buttoned from elbow to wrist, but might also be laced. If a paltock is not worn, or the seamstress wishes to strengthen the front fastening, (where there is considerable strain) a panel may be attached to one side of the opening and fastened with hook and eyes or snaps to the lining on the other side. Properly done, this should be invisible. The same process can be followed on the sleeve, but this is not usually necessary. The sleeves might be cut in one piece with the body section, but were probably inserted in the armhole as with modern sleeves. Again, this is a new style of construction (except for the brief tenure of the bliaut). If the garment is parti-quarterly, the sleeves can be divided in two parts to either match or contrast with the body part. The sleeve might be only half-length, showing the tight-buttoned paltock sleeve beneath; occasionally the sleeve would fall from the elbow to the ground, cut into fantastic foliated dagges, and the tippits would be cut off; in any case, tippits went out of fashion just after mid-century. The matching hood was also sewn parti-colored, with a long liripipe falling down the back; if this was longer than the floor, as was often the case, the end might be tucked into the hip belt to keep it from dragging.

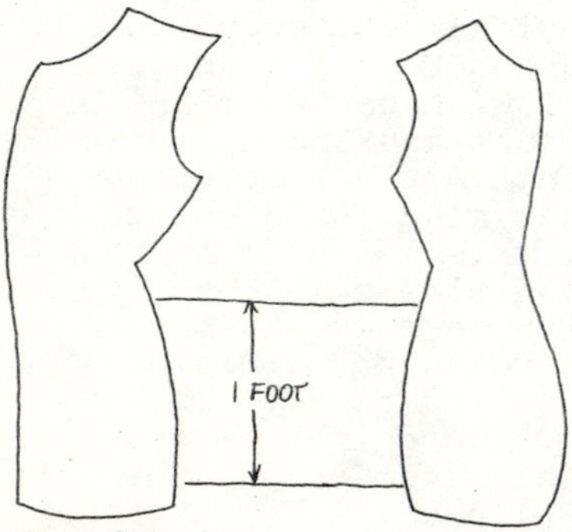

Half Front

Half Back

Cut of the Male Cotehardie

The circular mantle without arm-slits continued to be in fashion during this time. Sometimes, especially among the middle class, the skirt of the cotehardie was cut quite full and worn ankle-length. Coronation robes, however, continued to be on the old pattern: a series of loose tunics worn with the semi-circular cloak. Men's hair continued to be worn fairly short, reaching about the nape of the neck. It was parted in the center, and might be simply curled under in a "pageboy" style, or fixed in a curl around the bottom, thin at the forehead and widening into a full roll of hair at the back.

For women, the sideless surcote continued to be used, sometimes plain and sometimes decorated with the lady's armorial bearings. This became more of a ceremonial garment as time went on, and for general wear, the lady's cotehardie came into fashion. This was similar to the man's style, in having a very tight fit and fastening with buttons from neck to waist, and in having wrist-length tight buttoned sleeves. However, the lady's cotehardie widened abruptly from the hips into a very full skirt with wide gores, and had a very low, off-the-shoulder neckline. The woman's cotehardie might also have tippits and be particolored. The man's style of hip-belt was also worn with the woman's cotehardie; if it was not, there might be two vertical slits in the skirt front to help the lady raise the skirt when walking, and to allow her to reach a belt worn <u>beneath</u> the cotehardie, on which the lady carried her purse, keys and so forth. When the neck was very low, broaches might be worn on the shoulder pieces and in the center front to hold the garment in place securely. A lady's cotehardie was was also found in the diggings at Herjofsnes; this is shown on pg. 76, along with the cut of the sleeve. There are a number of mundane patterns cut in six pieces (front, back, two side fronts and two side backs) which can be easily adapted to imitate this authentic cut. Gores can be added as desired between the six sections of the skirt to increase the fullness. If you wish, the dress may be laced up the back or front from neck to waist and the buttons left off.

Gradually Curled Hair of a Fashionable Man

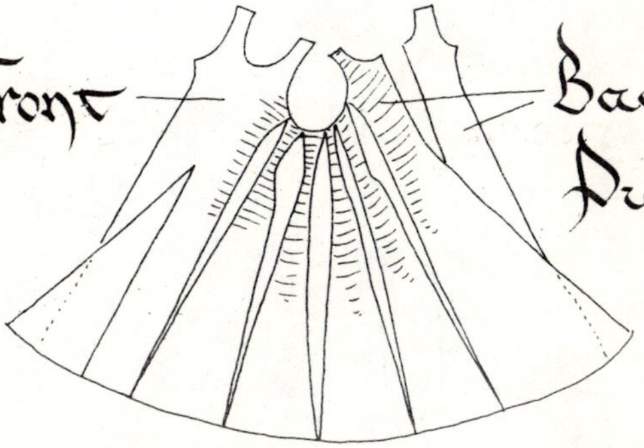

Cut of the Sleeve

Pieces showing the Danish cut of the Woman's Cotehardie

The neckline of the mundane pattern, if one is used, should be cut lower to correspond with the picture shown. Around the middle of the century, the ends of the sleeves were extended to the knuckle over the lady's han, but this might also be turned back to form a cuff. It is interesting that no sort of necklace was worn with the cotehardie; the neckline was left bare with most of the jewelry concentrated in the hip belt and headdress. The lady's cotehardie was parti-colored in all the same patterns as the men's version. Occasionally, less fashionable women wore a leather belt fastened around the hips like the metal ones, but with a long tongue hanging down at one side of the front.

The ceremonial sideless surcote was worn over the cotehardie for special occasions. The back panel at the top was left fairly wide, but the front panel was considerably reduced, sometime to no more than a handsbreath across. This was often covered by a <u>plastron</u> (a strip of fur) or edged with fur around the armholes. The narrow front and wide back panel allowed the lining (usually a rich fabric of a contrasting color)

to show as the lady walked. There was often a strip of jewelled trim down the center front which Norris believed was attached to the cotehardie beneath by hooks to hold the surcote in place. The jewelled belt was worn on the cotehardie under the surcote, and showed at the armholes on the sides. Some authorities believe that the sideless surcote was cut in one piece on the T-tunic pattern, but others believe that this later version had a separate skirt cut on the circle and attached to the top sections at the hips. The earlier type of sideless surcote might be cut shorter than the underskirt hem, but the later ceremonial one was almost always longer than floor length in front and extended into a longish train in the back.

Underwear for ladies did not change greatly with the advent of the cotehardie. Corsets continued to be worn, and indeed were now more necessary with the tightly fitted gown. There was evidently still some sort of shift, but with the very low neckline, some ladies of the current Middle Ages wear a full-length, full-skirted "slip" with thin spaghetti straps at the sides of the neckline or even a full half-skirt.

The various kinds of pelicon continued to be worn for warmth, along with circular and semi-circular cloaks. Another kind of surcote also used for warmth resembled the gowns of the earlier part of the century or a modern bathrobe. It was a loose, A-line robe, buttoned to the waist, with a plain round collar and full sleeves. These might be open, falling from the shoulder, or buttoned closed to the wrist. Since the fourteenth century was a period of great sophistication and personal vanity, a certain amount of make-up or "paint" was worn by both men and women of the court, although this was unusual in the Middle Ages among the respectable.

The wide, wimpled headdress montioned earlier was worn generally during the earlier part of the century. A transitional style was to braid a very wide plait reaching across the back of the head from temple to temple. A fillet was worn and a wimple which was fastened under the bottom edge of the braid. Tiny

The Surcote

curls lined the edge of the braid on the lower part and fell along the edge of the wimple there. If the wimple was worn on the outside of the dress's neckline it was called the guimpe. The other hair styles of the fourteenth century were also based on braids in various arrangements. They might be wound on each side of the head like the former ramshorn style, or wound around the head from bottom to top in a halo effect. The braids might also be folded once or twice like a segmented ruler or a road map at the sides of the head to make stiff vertical columns. These might be caught in circles attached to the sides of a coronet or encased in two metal mesh cylinders called templars attached to a fillet. Any of these styles might be covered by a light transparent veil. The crispine or hair-net was also used to cover the braids and hold them in place, or, occasionally, all the hair might simply be gathered in a massive bun at the nape of the neck and covered by the crispine. A miniature version of the hip-belt in small but elaborately decorated plaques was worn around the head as a circlet.

Ladies' shoes, being hidden by their skirts, were less elaborate than those of the men. This was the period when shoes were very pointed. An ordinary shoe resembled the one illustrated opposite and most ladies' shoes would be of this type. For more fashionable wear, the toes might be elongated a foot or more and stuffed with some substance to keep them rigid. Or they might be elongated greatly a yard or longer, and attached to the knee or even the waist-belt with fine chains. This last fashion was quite rare in England, used by only the most

extreme dandies. These shoes can be easily reproduced in heavy cloth or light leather using an old slipper as a pattern. The method of construction is detailed under the section titled "early Tudor Female Garb". The only difference is in the shape of the toes. The bottom line of the side piece of the shoe pattern should be extended straight out, and the top line gradually angled downward to meet the bottom at a point. The distance from toe to point of the shoes is largely up to the taste of the wearer.

Richard II, who reigned 1377-1399, was a gourmet and leader of fashion, and during his period garb definitely went to extremes. The short braes or slops sometimes disappeared entirely, and the hosen were sewn together to make something like a pair of modern tights with a codpiece attached. The codpiece, in this case, was a simple functional flap. The cotehardie at its most fashionable shrank to the hip-bone level, or about the length of the average man's mundane shirt. The jewelled hip-belt continued to be worn with this, although it was now only an inch or two above the hem, and the chest continued to be padded out by the pourpoint worn beneath. At first, the sleeves of this

Topical Shoe

garment continued to be tight to the wrist, and the only new feature was a high, stiff collar. This collar identified the style as the courtrepy, jaquette, anslet, or "new curtal weed." Although the garment could not have contained much more than three yards of material, the rich and fashionable paid fabulous sums for such courtrepies, heavily embroidered and decorated with jewels and gold. One in the possession of the Duc de Bourbon was valued at 4,200 gold crown, and Richard II wore another worth 30,000 marks. Sir Gawain and the Green Knight describes one such as "decked and bestuck with gems that glance away and there on were the birds of hill and dale cunningly needled, as the popinjay and trutes that sit preening through the summer's day and True-love knots that both were deft and fine." Somewhat later a variety of large sleeves were added to the courtrepy, either very wide, triangular, open sleeves, often dagged, or "bagpipe" sleeves which were tight on the forearm but formed huge closed bags at elbow level. Older and less fashionable men, who could not handle this style continued to wear loose robes and ganaches of the earlier period.

Fashionable Young Man's Courtrepy

At the other extreme from the courtrepy was the houpeland or houpplelande, which was contemporary with it. This was cut very full indeed, like a circular cape with sleeves, with a long train. It was made manageable by pleating it in folds held in place by a waist-belt. The man's houpeland had a high, stiff collar just like that of the courtrepy, which reached to the earlobe at the sides and often even higher in back.

A necklace was often worn at the base of the collar. The sleeves were cut in a rectangle, very full, open, and frequently dagged, reaching to the ground. The houpeland might have a small slit neckline, or be open all down the front and fastened with buttons. The side seams might also be left open to knee or thigh level. Short versions were worn : to the ankle (called "bastard") or to just below the knee (called "half-thigh"). These were used for riding or active pursuits, and were commonly slit up the front. Hoods and caps were worn, with or without the chaperon on top. Now that a more functional belt had returned, a purse (called an "escarcelle") and a small dagger or misericorde were often suspended from it. The purse was made like a rectangular envelope with a flap on the front.

Long Full Houpeland

Bells were often used as decoration, attached to the waist-belt, edging the hood cape, sewn to the dagges on the sleeves, or along the edges of a wide decorative badric worn over one shoulder, across the chest, and under the opposite arm. The cotehardie and/or padded pourpoint were worn under the houpeland. The undergarment might have tight sleeves or ones with full cuffs hanging down several inches. The fourteenth century was the hay-day of heraldry in garb. A family's badge or arms or even motto was frequently powdered all over the fabric of the houpeland, as it was appliqued on the sideless surcote and on the man's cyclas. An initial might also be used in this way.

As in most periods when high fashion was extreme and difficult to wear, in the fourteenth century the lower classes and the nobility in its moments of relaxation wore considerably different styles from those described above. Many simple folk wore long gowns virtually unchanged from those of the previous century, or even knee-length tunics for working. If a cotehardie style was worn, it was made mid-thigh to calf length, with a looser fit through the body and much fuller skirts. In the same way, the less extreme woman's cotehardie had a low round neckline but was still on the shoulder, and resembled a simple princess dress. The earlier form of the sideless surcote with a wide panel of plain cloth in front was also worn.

Citizen's Wear

Gentlewoman

From the Month of August
Tres Riches Heures of
Jean, Duc de Berry

The 15th Century

The fifteenth century continued and expanded the traits of the late fourteenth: the extravagance and imagination in men's garb and the sophistication and awareness of the body in women's dress. Fur grew ever more popular as trim, and figured fabric was once again common. Designs were now frequently large-scale and based on graceful scrolling plant forms. Occasionally a more rigid and conventional pattern appeared, foreshadowing the Tudor designs which followed.

During the first quarter of the century, costume continued almost unchanged, and indeed the houppelande in various modifications continued to be fashionable throughout the century. The skirt of the houpplande was somewhat narrowed for ordinary dress, and a band of decoration was frequently worn across the shoulders and chest just above the arms. The skirt travelled from above the knee to just below knee length to mid-shin, ankle, or floor length. The sleeves again might be bagpipe, or wide and triangular with or without dagges. The collar continued to be upstanding and round in most cases, although not always. In the period of Henry V, the skirt of the houppelande narrowed still further, until it was no more than a long robe, and a variety of collars were added: an upstanding V-shape, a flat rectangle like that of the woman's version, or a lower round neckline at the throat's base. Hair was now worn in a "bowl"cut as shown. The belt might be worn at the natural waist or low on the hips.

French Houpeland

During the first part of the century, ladies continued to wear the cotehardie and sideless gown, but within the first twenty-five years, the French fashion of ladies adopting the houppeland moved across the channel. It was exactly like the man's version, except for the collar, which was square and turned down flat on the shoulders. The belt on the ladies's houppelande was worn high, just under the bust. This first had a long tail, but later was simply a wide band around the waist. The first type of the remarkable fifteenth century reticulated headdresses appeared at this time. The hair was gathered above the ears in two buns held in place by a net bag, and a stuffed roll was placed over this. Often the sides of the stuffed roll were tipped up and the center portion bent down to a point on the forehead, creating a heart-shaped effect. Elaborate headdress was the most outstanding feature of fifteenth century women's garb, and while dress changed slowly, a gown can be dated quite exactly during this century by the headdress. This will be discussed in a separate section below.

Women's Houpeland Having Square Collar

Since this was the high point of the Italian Renaissance, it is not surprising that Italian fashions found their way north to England.

Among them was a kind of short overtunic, cut like a circular cloke but slit up the front on each side to shoulder level. The central panel was caught by a waist-belt, while the rest of the circle of cloth fell free. Another kind of garment based on this style was a knee-length tunic, triangular in shape. It was caught by a waist-belt into wide, heavy folds or pleats over the chest and skirt. Several styles of sleeve were used with this: full cylindrical one, "pokey" sleeves which were bag-pipe shaped but ended at the elbow, and wide tri-angular panels slit up to the shoulder to form hanging panels behind the arm. The skirt was frequently slit at the sides to the hip or waist, and it was common to outline wrists, skirt hem, and neckline with narrow bands of fur. The chaperon, which, as we have seen, was first simply a normal caped hood worn in a new way, was now made up in its completed form. This was a padded roll with an attached liripipe and a cockscomb, often folded into an upstanding shape stiffened with wire.

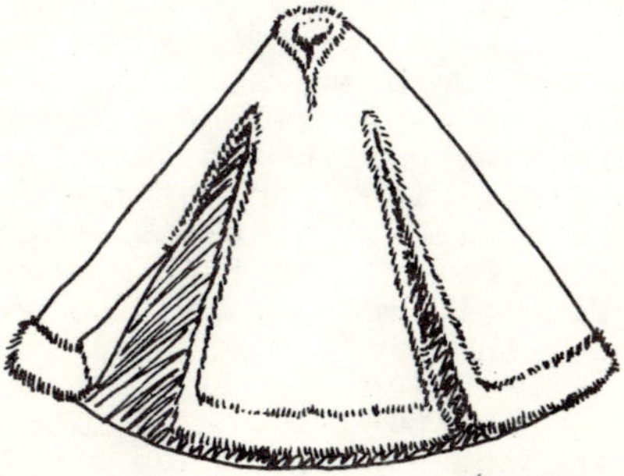

Diagram of Cloke-Tunic

A revival of the very short tunic recurred around 1450 in which this same style just mentioned was shortened to a few inches below the waist. The sleeves were padded slightly at the top, the beginning of a style which was to grow in the next few years. The neck was cut in a wide, shallow V-shape which showed the high collar of the pour-point underneath. This latter garment was now call-ed the "doublet". The vertical trend in men's garb reached its greatest popularity toward the end of the century. Padded sleeves much like the leg-o-mutton sleeves at the turn of the nineteenth century were added to the long, close robe which

which had evolved from the houppelande, and this was worn with a tall, brimless hat much like a truncated henin.

Diagram of Tunic

During the period from 1425-1450, the lady's houpplande underwent gradual modifications. The sleeves narrowed, becoming a straight, loose sleeve about a foot around at the wrist, and then straight and tight to the wrist with a cuff. The V-neck widened and deepened, spreading out onto the shoulders and down to the waist belt. During the transition period, the floor-length houpplande sleeves were sometimes worn with the deep, off the shoulder V-neckline. The front of the V was often filled in with a placket or higher under-dress of a contrasting color. By 1450 the skirt and bodice were definitely cut separately, with the seam hidden under the wide, tight belt which fitted below the bust. A lady in full court dress is shown on page 91, from 1450-1460, wearing this type of gown and the double-veiled henin. The deep V-neck appeared in both back and front, either with or without the placket in front. The most common trim was fur, often vair or miniver, added at neckline, wrist cuffs, and often in a deep band around the hem.

Both short and long garments were popular at the end of the fifteenth century, the reign of Richard III. The short, pleated tunic continued to be fashionable. It often had padded sleeves and chest, and the first signs of the slashing and bombasting favored in the next reign appear at this time. Thigh-length soft leather boots with spurs and pointed toes were worn with this style on occasion. The type of long robe in which Henry VII is usually shown had also now come into vogue. It was somewhat full, open all the way up the front with wide, pointed revers folded back at the neckline, and was held at the waist by a belt. The sleeves had an opening at elbow length for the hand to pass through, and the whole was trimmed with fur, or possibly lined with fur throughout. This type of gown can easily be made from a slightly modified mundane bathrobe pattern.

Another fashionable short garment was the journade. This was cut like the circular cloke, but reached only to the top of the thighs. It might be closed or open up the front. Any of the fashionable sleeves might be attached, and it was also often trimmed with fur. With it were worn an odd little hat like an upside-down flower pot with a fur brim, hosen with pointed toes, and poulaines or wooden sandals worn to keep feet out of the mud. The journade was the ancestor of the Tudor man's coat popular during the period of Henry VIII, when the front and neckline sections were turned back to make a wide collar and revers.

The Gothic Man

The last innovation in women's garb during the fifteenth century was the "round dress" which led into early Tudor style. It had a moderately full skirt which fell with almost no folds in a cone to the floor. The sleeves were straight and tight, and the neckline had a low, circular shape which did not descend to the belt. The lower section of the decollete was filled in with an arc of fabric called a plastron, although it did not resemble the item of the same name worn on the sideless surcote. The first square-cut neckline, forerunner of the following style, appeared around 1480. The dress was otherwise very similar to the cotehardie, but had a new kind of girdle. It was worn lower on the hips; the two ends of the section passing around the body were joined at the side front by three short pieces set in a triangle with a small piece of decorative metal at each angle. From the bottom of the triangle, a long tongue fell down, ending in some decorative article such as a purse.

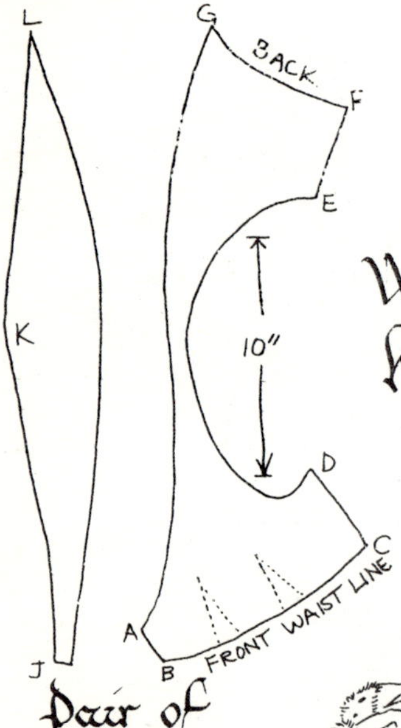

Pair of Bodices

Women's Houpeland

Hairdressing and headdresses were quite varied during the fifteenth century. At the first part of the era, men's hair was worn in the peculiar style shown earlier which looked much like a mushroom cap of hair. A slightly longer version, about to ear level, appeared in the reign of Henry VI, and about 1460 it became fashionable to let the hair grow down to the shoulder. Beards were not popular during the entire period, and indeed did not return to fashion until the time of Henry VIII. Many kinds of hats were worn, most falling into one of two main styles. One was the upright sometimes brimless type mentioned above, shaped like a flowerpot, a sugarloaf, or a baby's pacifier. The other was a "Robin Hood" hat with a brim bent into a sharp triangular shape, high around the back and coming down to a low point over the forehead in front. The crown was quite high, and might be also triangular, round, or similar to the sugarloaf style, In the the 1460's a new hat was introduced called the bonnet, which evolved into the Tudor man's hat. This had a round, moderately high crown and a stiff upturned brim slightly lower all around it.

The Journade

Woman's headgear was even more fanciful. The headdress of the early fifteenth century evolved from the templars worn in the preceeding reigns: two bags of net or cylinders of metal mash encasing the hair on each side of the face. The idea of this headdress was width, while the later henin styles were vertical. The side pieces of the reticulated headdress, as this was called, were generally shaped like a truncated cone or half-circle, flat at the end and the side against the head. These rigid little boxes were attached to a fillet around the head. A veil could be attached in several ways to this foundation: with a circlet, a long veil tucked in at the edges of the templars on each side of the forehead, or a veil draped over wires tilting up at each end in an arc from the edge of the templar. This last might be worn with or without a circlet. During the reign of Henry VI, the next development of this style appeared in the heart-shaped headdress already described. The side cauls were made in one or two half-circles or half-cones which might be stuffed with the lady's own hair, or if this were insufficient, made over a rigid foundation. These cauls rose quite high on each side of the head, and the padded roll was placed over them in the shape already described. About 1440 a long liripipe was added, taken from the men's style. Sometimes an entirely different shape was created by angling both sides of the padded roll backward and sharply upward together at about a forty-five degree angle. The padded roll was occasionally replaced by a rich and elaborate circlet of metal and jewelry which looked very striking indeed.

The Round Dress

The reticulated headdress went out of high fashion about 1465-70, but middle class women in particular continued to wear their version of the style for some time. In this the hair or padding was arranged in two divisions of about the same shape and size as the cauls in the previous reticulated headdress. A rectangular piece of fabric about thirty by sixteen inches was brought around the head and over the ears with two corners sticking up in front. (See the picture that follows on page 95). These corners are marked A and B in the picture. The middle top of the back section was pulled to the forehead and pinned to the two ends there. A cloth version of the reticulated cauls was thus created, and over this was pinned another veil which hung down at the back. A rigid version of this was also worn, made out of richer material, which much resembled a bivalve shell in shape, and had a much finer transparent veil attached to the back and sides. After the fall of Constantinople in 1453, it became a rather macabre vogue to wear headdresses almost exactly like Turkish turbans, although this particular style was more popular in Italy than in the rest of Europe Various kinds of hoods were also worn, shaped like the early type of man's hood, but without the cape on the shoulders.

The style most closely associated with the V-necked gown was the henin. This is a simple style to make, being no more than a cone, like an ice-cream cone or a dunce cap, rolled of a stiff substance (say cardboard) and covered with fabric.

This basic design was complicated in several ways. At first, one transparent veil of soft fabric was draped along the full length of the henin and over the forehead to about eyebrow level. Around 1450 a set of two veils was adopted, attached to a wire framework shaped like two V's joined at each side point to point: The first set of V's ran from the front to the tip of the henin; the second set started about half-way back and rose two or three inches higher from the henin. Around 1460 the design changed again. First a piece of fine transparent lawn was draped over the head, reaching down to eyebrow level in front. Next a band of black velvet about five by thirty inches was placed over the lawn, and a small second piece was attache at the back to hang down a bit below the shoulders. On top of this was the henin itself, and the front of the velvet band was turned back and pinned to the center front of the henin and the sides with a jewel. A soft transparent veil was then thrown over the henin to hang down a few inches beyond the tip. If the wearer were entitled to a coronet, it was worn at the base of the henin just above the velvet band.

Around 1470 the butterfly headdress appeared. The henin shrank to a smaller, conical cap with a flat top, similar to a fez. This was first worn just like the henin, pulled down on the forehead to hide the hair and draped with a soft veil. Then the cap was brought back until it covered only the back of the head, at about the angle a yarmulke is worn. A wire framework was attached which reached out in front of the headdress to form a point on the forehead, then angled back and up to pass over two wires attached to the top back of the headdress. The two wires were shaped much like a butterfly's antennae, hense the name. From the antennae, the veil fell straight down to shoulder level. The veil was cut in a modified L-shape, so that the sides of the henin were covered only about half-way down.

Shoes continued to be of the same general shape as during the fourteenth century: fitted fairly closely to the shape of the foot but with pointed toes. The point lengthened to its maximum in 1460, then returned to almost normal by 1480. The shoe might be cut low like a bedroom slipper and slipped on over the foot, or it might be ankle high, either open with a point at the front and back of the ankle, or fastened tightly around the ankle and laced down the side there. As mentioned, knee or thigh-high boots were also worn. To protect the shoe and support the long toes, a wooden clog was used, called poulaine or <u>galouche</u>.

Hood

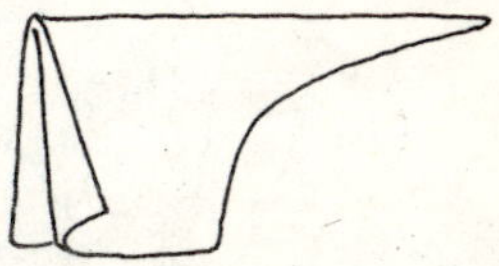

Jewelry also became more popular and more elaborate during the fifteenth century. Necklaces returned: women wore delicate designs, often open and lacy, with pendant jewels or interwoven styles. Men wore heavier styles, especially the well-known collar of SSS shapes. Anything possible was adorned with jewelry: brooches were added to hats and other garments; mantles were fastened with rich <u>tasseaux</u> or round metal ornaments with holes for decorative cords to pass through, or with bands of jeweled metalwork.

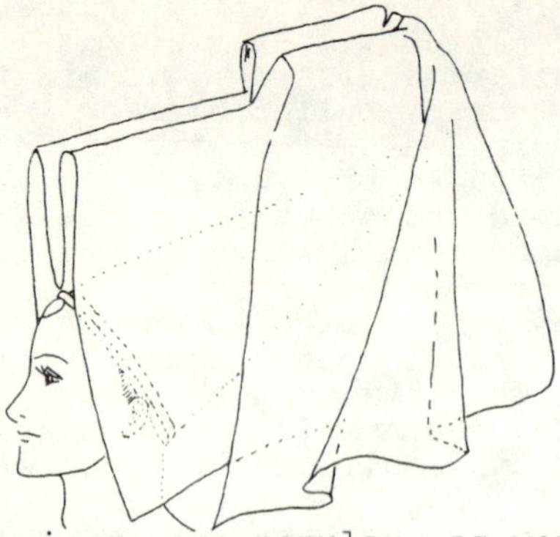

Finger rings were popular, as were pendants, reliquaries, and jeweled purse fastenings and girdles. Crown and coronets were elaborate and massive.

Again, however, the dress of the lower orders was quite different from that of the high nobility. This was to be a continuing and growing characteristic of garb in Europe from the late fourteenth century up until the twentieth. The uniformity which had prevailed in general shape and style of clothes from one class to the next during the first seven centuries of our period was now lost.

A distinct and self-conscious middle class had now emerged as well, creating a middle style of clothing between rich and poor. This middle class wore simplified versions of the high style. Instead of the full houppelande, they wore moderately full gowns, long, calf-length or knee-length, with any of the sleeve styles mentioned above. The circular garment with the separate front panel was also used, and a simple, fairly close-fitting tunic reaching to mid-thigh. Peasants continued to wear the same loose knee-length tunic and hood as for the last four centuries.

Women also imitated the styles of the upper class as best they could. For the first part of the century, the middle-class woman wore a less-extreme version of the cotehardie, with a less-full skirt just reaching the ground and a scooped neckline which still remained on the shoulders. Less fashionable women continued to wear wimples and caped hoods. Later middle-class women wore full dresses with V-necks, but, although they reached to the waist-belt, they were quite narrow and on the shoulders, and were always filled in by an undergarment. Towards the end of the century the square neckline also appeared on middle-class dresses. Lower-class women wore simple ankle-length dresses with plain round necklines slit down the front, or a shallow round or V-shape. Occasionally, peasant women might wear a separate skirt and top with perhaps a short-sleeved "sweater" reaching to the waist over them. Middle and lower class women copied the elaborate headdresses of the upper class as best they could. The bourgeoisie might have a simple reticulated style, a padded roll, or a henin-like cap with a veil; the peasant was content with a hood or a simple opaque veil thrown over the head.

Henry VIII
after the Eworth painting

Early Male Tudor Garb

As with female Tudor garb, the description of early male Tudor garb is complicated by an embarassment of riches and the growth of specialized costume. We have a vast amount of written material from this period in letter, descriptions, household accounts, and wills which describe the clothing of all classes in minute detail. For a variety of reasons, clothing had begun to change more rapidly, and within ten or fifteen years major developments might take place. Also nations and regions like France, Italy, Germany and Spain were beginning to develop quite individual styles, and each of these "national" styles influenced English costume and was influenced by it in turn. In earlier days different professions and groups had worn garb with distinctions which were obvious to their contemporaries, as we can clearly see in a work like the Canterbury Tales. By Tudor times we have voluminous records of the distinguishing clothing which was worn by social classes (peasant, workman, apprentice, merchant, etc.) or by professional groups (clergy, military, lawyer, doctor of medicine, etc.) as well as high-style and less fashionable people in general. This being so, we can obviously cover only a small segment of the available material in a short general chapter like this one.

During the early part of the century (ca. 1510) the basic undergarments consisted of waist-high hosen ("tights") with a cod-piece like a plain flap fastened with laces, and a shirt of very fine lawn or linen, invariably white. The shirt had a fairly low round or square neckline tied shut with a lace, and was cut very full in the body and sleeves. The area all around the neckline was pleated and smocked into a sort of yoke, including across the top of the sleeves, which were attached in the manner shown in the diagram following.

If you are using a mundane shirt pattern, be sure to get a "peasant" style and be careful to make it full enough, for much of the stylish effect of cuttes and slashing depended on drawing out smalll puffs of the shirt fabric through the cuttes. In some cases where the cuttes were very small (as on the front of the doublet) or it was not practical for some reason to pull the under fabric out, artificial puffs were sewn to the underside of the surface to protrude through the holes. This was generally a late style, however. The neckline

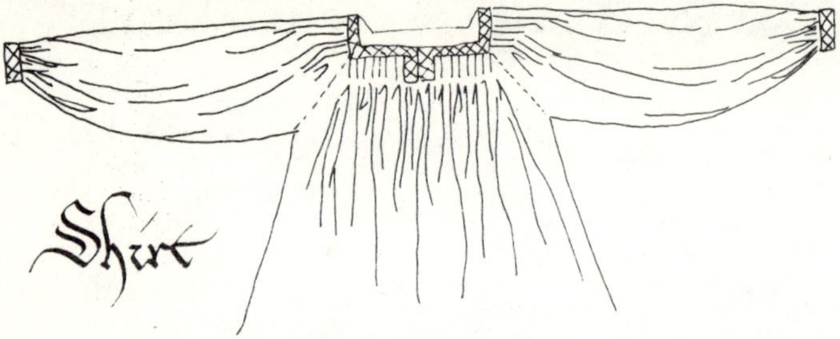

Shirt

and the frill of fabric gathered at the wrist were frequently heavily embroidered with blackwork; an example of a pattern used at this time can be seen in the chapter on women's Tudor garb. As the century wore on, the neck of the shirt rose ever higher, at last evolving into the Elizabethan ruff, but until that period the neckline was always cloth, not lace, although the high, gathered ruff looked very similar. Fine shirts were a major element in good costume, and even noble ladies often made shirts for their families.

English Noble wearing a Simar

Over the shirt was worn the pourpoint or paltock, the same garment described by that name in the chapter on fifteenth century dress. It might be closed in front like a very short (waist-length) tunic; the bottom of the shirt often showed under the edge of the paltock in a little puff around the waist. More often the pourpoint was open down the front; it might be fastened diagonally across the chest, or might be open in a wide decreasing "V" with or without laces drawn loosely across the front of the shirt. The area between the shirt and the pourpoint was often covered by the <u>plackard</u>, a male version of the stomacher worn with the lady's V-necked gown. A variety of sleeves were worn with the pourpoint, either attached at the shoulder or laced into the armhole with points. Many of these sleeves were open in some way, such as divided at the elbow into two sections, left open up the back seam, or slashed in a design. Sometimes a type of sleeve would be worn which was open in a gradually increasing bell shape until it was quite full at the wrist. Another style which was revived from the earlier period was puffed at the shoulder like a leg-o-mutton sleeve, then tight down the forearm to the wrist.

Another English Nobleman wearing another Simar

As a top garment, there might be added a long robe called the simar. This was cut in a circular shape, so that the top front edges which would otherwise overlap almost to the opposite shoulder on each side could be turned back to form wide revers at the neckline. The sleeves might be small bells or, frequently, long tubular hanging shapes with a hole for the arm to pass through at the elbow. The simar might be full-length or might be cut off at mid-thigh to make a short surcote, although even when the body was short the sleeves were left at almost ankle length. Occasionally the sleeve might be attached at the back of the shoulder only, making falling "wings" behind the arm. Both the these garments can be created by simple adaptations of mundane patterns: for the pourpoint a vest pattern is the obvious answer, or a shirt pattern if you need to adapt the sleeves. The simar is almost identical to a modern bathrobe, with the front center line extended so that it can be turned back for the revers.

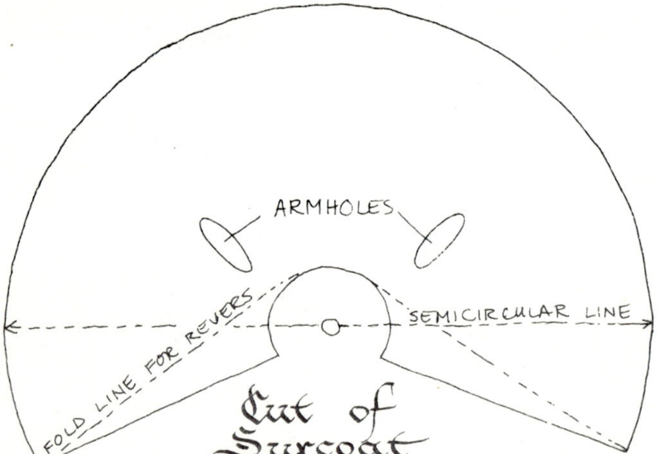

Cut of Surcoat

During this century the head was almost never bare indoors or out. The most popular hat this early period was a low-crowned, wide-brimmed style rather like the type worn for motoring by the ladies in the early twentieth century. A picture of it can be seen on a preceeding page. An interesting kind of cloak was also worn at this time, particularly for riding. Its cut can be seen in the illustration on the next page. The sections marked

D and E in the diagram covered the thighs of the wearer while he was on horseback. This cloak was worn either in the usual fashion with the center opening falling down the front, or draped around the figure leaving one arm uncovered. In the latter case the neckline was held under the right arm and the right-hand section labelled "D" was thrown over the left shoulder; the part marked "C" (the other side of the neckline) was then tucked into the top of the front to hold the entire cloak in place.

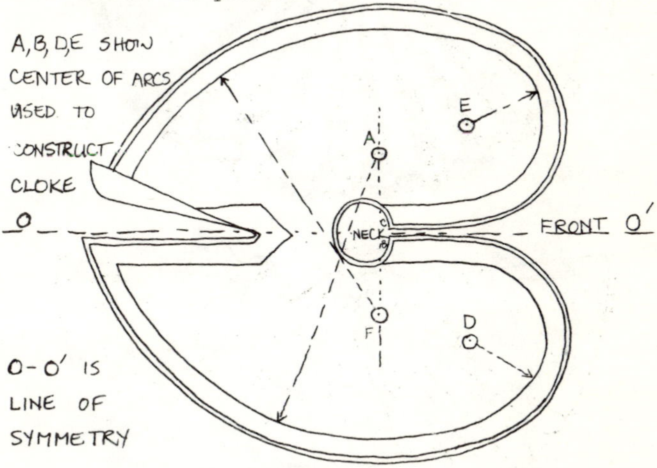

A garment which emigrated from Italy, worn with either civil dress or armour, was a type of skirt called the <u>base</u> or <u>bases</u>. A particularly gorgeous example in cloth of gold and cloth of silver was worn by Henry VIII at the field of the Cloth of Gold. The bases were a three-quarters of a circle tied around the waist with laces (or sometimes attached to the base of the pourpoint). Either the entire garment or the front section was formed into a series of padded pleats made by sewing a thick lining material between the two layers and quilting it with vertical lines radiating from the top to the bottom slightly so as to be wider at the bottom. The pleats might be more than one half inch thick. If the entire base was not quilted into pleats, the flat section at each side of the back closing was quilted in the usual way, as is clearly seen in the illustration following. The inside of the skirt had two strips of tape set across the width of the pleats to hold them in place. The bases might be made in all one fabric, but two materials were often used, to create a striped effect with each pleat being in an alternating fabric. It was quite usual to have a border at the lower hem, which would be counterchanged at each pleat, as seen below.

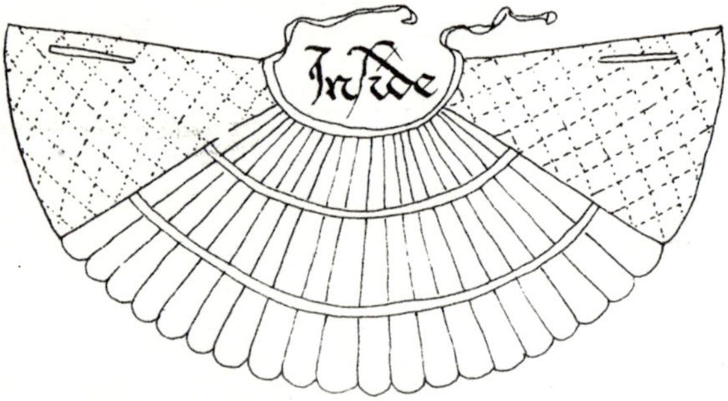

During the reign of Henry VII, beards were not fashionable in England, although they were more popular on the Continent. When worn they were generally quite close, covering the entire lower cheek area and chin, along with a small mustache across the upper lip but not drooping below it. Hair was worn fairly long, varying from just below chin level to slightly below shoulder level. Usually there was a short fringe across the forehead and the sides and back fell smoothly to be turned under at the ends in a "pageboy" style. Occasionally, longer hair might be dressed in several long vertical curls. The wide, flat hat described earlier was worn over a skull cap or coif. This coif might also be worn alone, an Italian fashion; it was made as an open network of cords decorated with jewels at the intersections, or a round cap similar to a beanie, or even a very odd type of cap with a section on one side cut out which looked for all the world like half a grapefruit or a large tomato worn upside-down on top of the head. Another popular hat was the French bonnet. This was made in the same way as the bonnet described in the chapter on fifteenth century garb: a round, moderately high crown with a plain, stiff, round brim turned up slightly lower than the crown all the way around. The brim was treated

in a variety of ways: it might be shaped higher on one side than the other, cut in a border around the top edge, or left open for a section and laced together with cords either from one side of the open section to the other, or laced through the brim all the way around. Buttons, broaches, or, rarely, ostrich feather, were often added as decorations around the brim. The bonnet was most often made in black velvet, but was also found in any coordinating color to match the wearer's costume. A similar type of round cap was made of felt, but was blocked into points on top. often four ridges like a cross over the crown. The brim, of the same kind as the French bonnet, began at the temple on each side and continued around the back.

The long, pointed effect in shoes, as in clothing generally, disappeared at the beginning of the sixteenth century, to be replaced by an emphasis on width. Fashionable shoes were often cut out over the instep with a strap just below the ankle, and the back was also cut quite low. Some shoes were designed like slippers or even backless mules with very wide rounded toes. A type of knee-length stocking, usually of linen, was sometimes worn to protect the hose. Both long and short boots were worn, from calf high to above the knee. These were often of very soft leather which formed folds about the leg, and were decorated with cuttes at times by the wealthy.

Rich and massive jewelry was popular during this period, although less so than during the reign of Henry VIII. Collars were popular, formed of a series of alternating shapes such as roses or knots, or heraldic symbols such as the portcullus.

Flocked Felt Hat

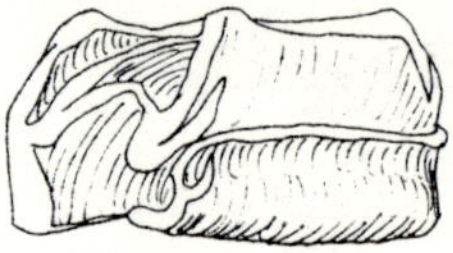

Massy chains were common with all classes which could afford them, made of heavy link shapes. These were worn like a baldric across the chest and under the opposite arm (this was known as "prisoner fashion"), or wound around the neck and shoulders several times,or laid across the shoulders Chains were given to signify an office, such as chancellor. Large jewelled or enamel broaches decorated hats, or were worn as pendants or reliquaries, and massive rings were worn sometimes one on every finger of the hand. It was a custom to slit the fingers of stylish gloves in cuttes so that a ring worn on the finger under the glove would show through it. Gloves were worn with almost any costume, some quite elaborate with gold lace and embroidery, others very plain and servisable.

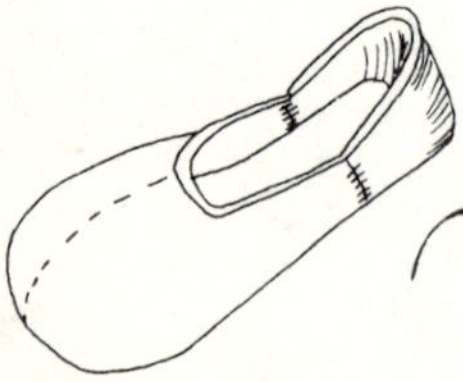

Tudor Shoes

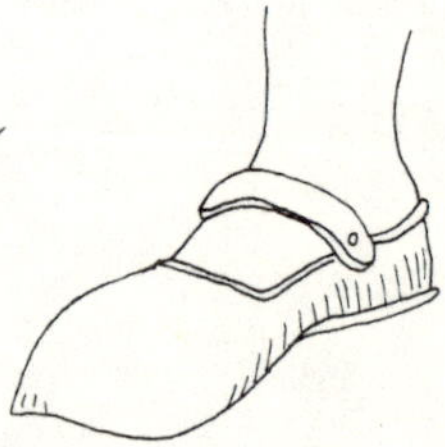

The reign of Henry VIII was definitely one of the most flamboyant periods of male attire in all of history. Henry himself was considered the most handsome noble figure of Europe on his accession in 1509, a distinction of which he was very proud. The fact that Henry was very vain about his well-shaped leg probably influenced the shortening of all garments to above the knee.

As mentioned previously, French influence was important in women's Tudor garb, especially since Henry's sister had married the French king and Anne Boleyn had spent some time at the court there. But Francis I of France was himself greatly influenced by Italian and German fashions. Bases were designed in a variety of interesting patterns, using counterchanging stripes matched on pourpoint and bases or divided quarterly.

Italian Bases

Both Italian and German fashion used the new idea of cuttes. Since Italian upper garments seldom reached below the waist, hosen were correspondingly important. They were slashed in many different patterns: the area from waist to thigh might be cut in long vertical lines or in a grid of wide square shapes. The design might be extended to the knees, or only a portion (say the thigh area) might be decorated. Sometimes only one leg would be slashed and the other left plain. A contrasting color fabric was allowed to show through the cuttes. But the length from knee to foot was always plain and close-fitting, although it might be of a patterned fabric.

The ultimate fashion in cuttes was created by the Landesknechten, German or Swiss mercenary soldiers. Legend has it that during the invasion of Swiss territory by Charles le Temeraire, Duke of Burgundy, in 1475-6, the Landesknechten utterly routed the Burgundian forces and, seizing the Duke's brightly colored silk pavilians cut them up to patch their ragged garments. The style was deliberately imitated out of admiration for the brave warriors, and a bizarre effect was created in which no two parts of the costume matched. One example of a Landesknecht pictured in contemporary sources showed him in a doublet with two rows of short vertical slashes and sleeves cut in panes or strips gathered at upper arm, elbow, and wrist. One sleeve is scarlet and the other purple with white and gold lining respectively. One upper leg of the hosen is bright blue, cutte in spirals over yellow, while the other is bright green cutte in long puffed panes like the sleeves over white. The netherstockings are, respectively, red and white vertical stripes and solid blue. In his broad-brimmed hat are long ostrich feathers in white, scarlet, gold, blue, and purple. As is obvious from this description, the total effect was startling to say the least, especially since the Landesknechten usually chose the various fabrics used from the brightest and most clashing colors possible.

A civilian adaptation is shown in Norris, worn by Francis I of France, consisting of a turquoise blue surcote trimmed with gold, a plackard and full puffed sleeves of black, gold, and white striped material slashed over white, a pink doublet, and hose of purple with white horizontal bars slashed over purple on one side and blue with diagonal gold stripes slashed over white above and black and white vertical stripes below on the other side, along with bright yellow shoes. The king also wears a purple undercap and a black velvet bonnet trimmed with a white ostrich plume. One hesitates to call a king's clothing absurd, but this outfit certainly strains the limits of tact. Luckily,these more extreme styles were seldom seen except among the most fashionable dandies.

The high style of the mid-1530's is well represented by the famous portrait of Henry VIII by Hans Eworth now at Trinity College Cambridge, showing the king at the age of fifty-one. The king wears from the inside outward: a shirt of fine white lawn or silk of the kind described above. The example in the picture has the small turned-down Peter Pan collar favored by the king, but might also have a high ruffled collar. The edge of the collar and cuffs was often overcast with a thin border of black silk thread in buttonhole or blanket stitch, and might in addition have a wide or narrow border of blackwork embroidery in black (obviously) or once in a while in red or gold. The lower half of the royal person was dressed in slops and hosen. The slops were similar to a modern pair of shorts (of the kind for exterior wear, not underwear), and were often decorated with cuttes or puffs. A shirt and slops was worn alone for hot sport such as a fast game of tennis. The hosen were attached to the slops with laces and points. These two garments were later known as the upperstockings and neatherstockings.

A closed pourpoint or doublet as it was now called, of the kind described above, came next. This usually had sleeves of the same material as the body attached or laced at the shoulder. This

Shirt & Slops

doublet, and especially the sleeves, was often decorated with cuttes, and among the wealthy it was fashionable to have the open seam created by one or more long vertical cuttes, or the back seam of the sleeve left open, held together with a series of small matching jewels. In the king's portrait the sleeves are slit full length four or five times with each slit held together with four jewels. The center front of the doublet is decorated by a band of contrasting material and the center opening is held together by four larger jewels. On each side of this center panel are several vertical bands of small cuttes with the shirt puffing through them. Below the end of the sleeve the ruffled cuff of the shirt can be seen.

Over the doublet is a vest, in a wide U-shape, and attached to this is a modified type of base. In this style the pleats were not padded as heavily, and the effect was exactly that of a very full pleated skirt. The skirt was open up the front and a padded cod-piece, attached to the slops beneath, often showed through the opening. The vest and skirt was frequently left out of the costume. In that case the doublet was cut with a skirt, much less full, so that the whole looked like a plain tunic open all the way down the front. The open section of the doublet then allowed the shirt to show down to the waist, and in this case the whole front of the shirt was often decorated with blackwork. A sash made of a thin white piece of cloth might be worn around the waist to hold the doublet closed (sometimes a regular belt took its place), and a dagger could be suspended from it.

Vest and Skirt

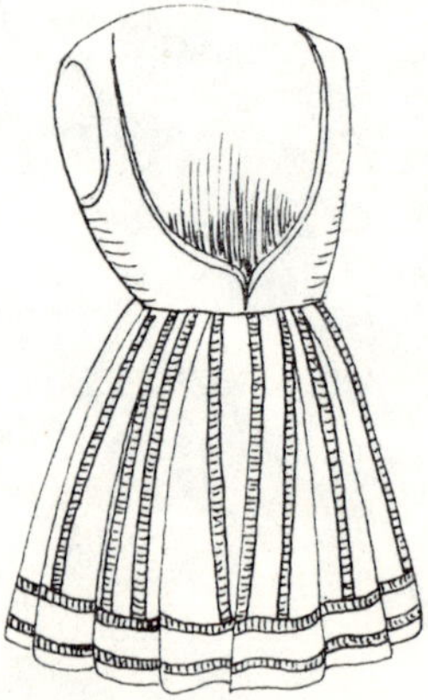

Over the whole was worn the surcote. This is the only garment whose construction should cause any real problems to the moderately experienced sewer. A diagram is shown on the next page. The basic design is similar to the simar in front; that is, it is cut so that the front two sections are extended, then turned back to form wide revers. In this style the revers are extended right around the back of the neck to make a square collar. The surcote was often lined with fur so that the turned back sections would thus appear to be a fur collar. The sleeve was basically the same tube with a slit for the arm, but the top of the sleeve is pushed up into a puff and stuffed with padding; this puff is fixed in place by a band around the upper arm of the sleeve. The opening FF is cut into a scalloped shape and turned down behind the elbow. The rest of the tubular sleeve falls down behind the arm in the usual way. This is rather hard to see because the sleeve is lost in the full folds of the surcote skirt. The back section of the surcote is cut in a semi-circular oval, then the shoulder section on each side is pleated into a smaller area (so that the finished surcote appears to be almost perfectly semi-circular), which makes the back of the surcote fall in deep folds. As a variation, the top of the sleeve would be made full and puffed as in the first style, but the bottom tubular section was omitted and the sleeve reached only to the elbow.

The French bonnet, now with a slightly higher and wider brim, was usually decorated with jewels and often with an ostrich plume. With square-toed shoes it completed the costume. In his old age, Henry wore a loose long robe like a caftan, but this could not be said to be a fashionable garment. A novelty which appeared at this time was clothing for nightwear, since previously people had slept naked. The nightshirt was exactly what the name suggests, the same sort of shirt worn during the day, but worn at night as the only garment. With it was worn a close-fitting cap like a baby bonnet which was known as a night-bonnet or biggin. A sort of loose dressing gown, very much like a modern wrap-over full-length robe was worn in private chambers for undress, and was called a nightgown. Anne Boleyn had one made of velvet lined with taffeta, both black, and trimmed with sable.

Hats and shoes continued in much the same fashion as before, both tending to flatness and width. The French bonnet has already been dis-

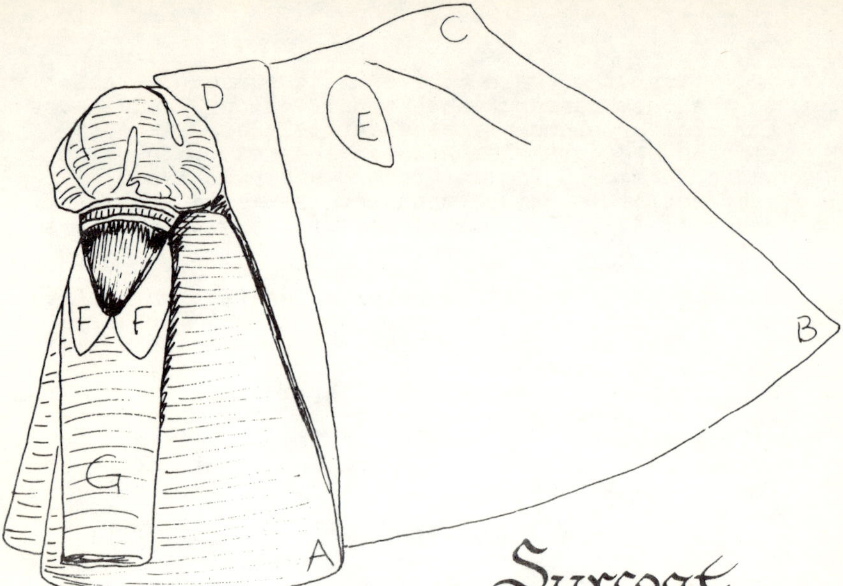

Surcoat Open Showing the Construction

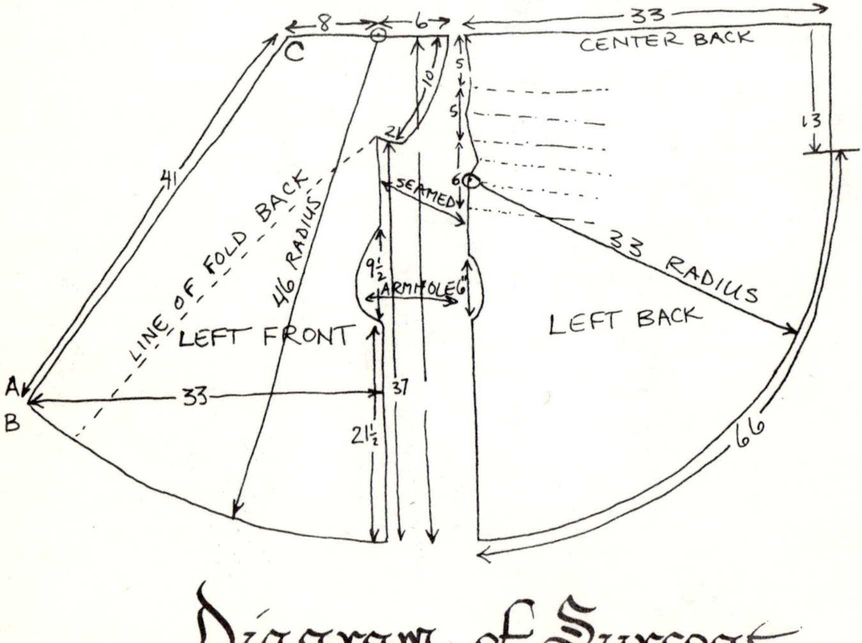

Diagram of Surcoat

cussed. A variation on this was the "flat cap", which was a sort of beret with a stiff round thin brim like a plate and a flat round crown. When laid down on a surface, the hat was perfectly flat, hence its name. Since it was an easy hat to make and wear, it soon became a favorite of the lower classes, and the term "Goodman Flatcap" became a contemptuous term of snobbery for the poorer classes. However, the hat was first worn for some time by the nobility. To distinguish their hats, the rich tilted the cap to one side of the head and decorated the underside of the brim with rich jewels. This is the type of hat Henry VIII is usually shown wearing. Each country had its distinctive style of hat: the Mullan cap, was much like the French bonnet in design, but was heavily decorated with festoons of pearls, feathers jewels, etc. It was worn over a net undercap. The French style was very close to the flat, and the Flemish version was similar to a highly exaggerated version of the same basic design. The hat worn by the Emperor Maximillian shows the brim cut in sections which overlap at the corners and give an effect somewhat like a flattened tricorn design; the style worn by the Compte de Flandre (Charles V) is obviously nothing more than a gigantic flat cap. The German style is also flat, but the brim is cut and folded in an interesting way which gives an entirely different effect to the final picture.

Shoes continued to be square-toed throughout the reign of Henry VIII; the usual shape was a rectangle with the toe end cut straight across. Shoes for court wear were often made of fine cloth and Henry himself favored white velvet (certainly the ultimate triumph of style over function). They were decorated with cuttes and even with jewels, as in the style shown on a following page. The section over the instep might be cut out in a square, and sometimes nothing was left of the top of the shoe except a toe-cap. Later in the period the ends of the toe were extended to the sides, first in small "ears" and later in fairly sizable rectangular extension which made the ends of the toe look like the head of a hammerhead shark. Heel-less mules continued to be worn for indoors, and for hard riding or outdoor work, high boots up to the thigh were used, still decorated with cuttes or other designs.

The jewelry of the time was massive, ornate, and showy, with a certain resemblance to badly designed modern costume jewelry, except that among the upper class it was all real. With the dissolution of the monasteries, vast quantities of jewels and precious metals which had been held by the Church for centuries were released into private hands. Before the sixteenth century, jewels were set "cabochon"- polished but not cut in facets. After 1475 jewels began to be cut either faceted, or in the case of the most valuable ones "table cut" rectangular on top with bevelled edges and a triangular underside. Massive collars and chains (worn across the shoulders) continued to be popular, and a variety of small designs were worn on the

Flemish hat

hat brim. These included ensignes, often large broaches with personal or symbolic designs, which evolved from the pilgrim's badges which had been worn in the hat on medieval times. Many other small purely decorative, items were added: beads, small jewels, braid, and tiny figures much like those worn on the traditional Tyrolean Alpenhut. Finger rings were large, and matched sets of small jewels used to hold together the slashes on sleeves were found in almost every jewelry wardrobe. A variety of large and elaborate pendants were worn, often in the shape of initials; this seems to have taken the place of the reliquaries and crucifixes which disappeared with the Reformation.

German hat

The decorative patterns of the Tudor period were less graceful and naturalistic than those of the fifteenth century, and consisted mainly of geometric, semi-naturalistic, and interlaced style. Vegetation was treated in a somewhat angular and formal style, close to the designs for modern crewelwork which are labelled "Jacobean". Natural subjects were occasionally treated naturalisticly, a foreshadowing of the later Elizabethan fashion, but this was rare in costume embroidery at this time. The interlace patterns came ultimately from early Celtic styles preserved in Wales, the origin of the Tudor family, and were extensively used as borders, panels, and so on. Lace of the modern type, an evolution of cut-work and embroidery, was beginning to be seen in the early Tudor period, but did not figure prominently in costume until the Elizabethan, and even more the Cavalier period.

The middle and lower classes, as mentioned above, did not really approximate the garb of the upper class very closely. Most professional men such as doctors, lawyers, etc., wore long robes to the floor, ungirdled, with wide loose sleeves. This robe might have a high round collar, or a wide collar turned down over the shoulders much like the simar worn during the first part of the last reign. The upper gentry, as was usual, wore a less elaborate variation on the fashionable style. This was mainly the shirt, doublet with skirt, and a less elaborate type of surcote with plain tubular sleeves slit vertically at the elbow. Upper level retainers such as pages, and the average citizen who was neither rich nor poor wore the shirt, slops and hosen, and over this the doublet with skirt, eliminating the surcote entirely. The sleeves might be straight and fairly tight, or elbow length. The neck was cut square, or occasionally round with a slight point in front, buttoned or laced down the front. The French bonnet and square-toed shoes completed the costume. A plain belt was often worn around the waist. The peasantry continued to wear something very like the tunic of past centuries: knee-length, loose, and straight in the body, with plain straight sleeves. The neck might have a buttoned fastening or a small turned-down collar.

Embroidery Patterns

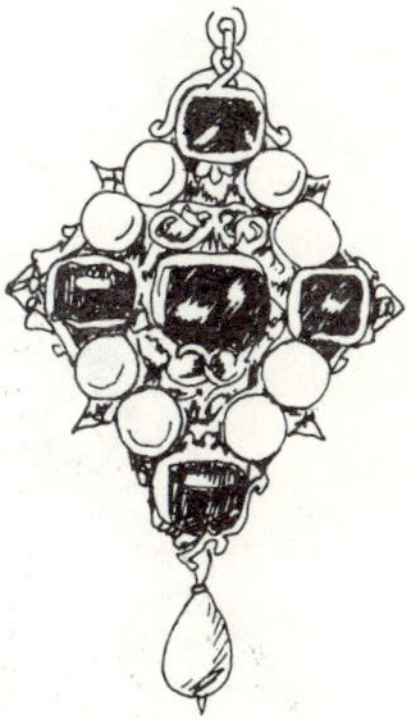

Typical Jewelry

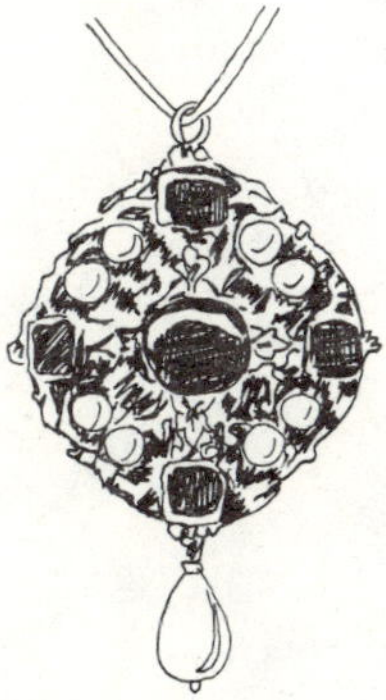

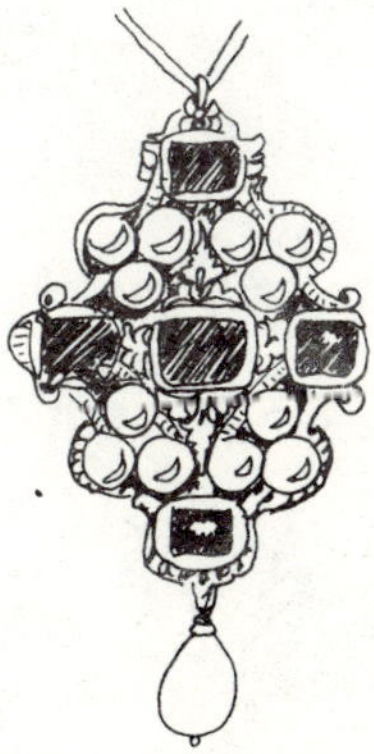

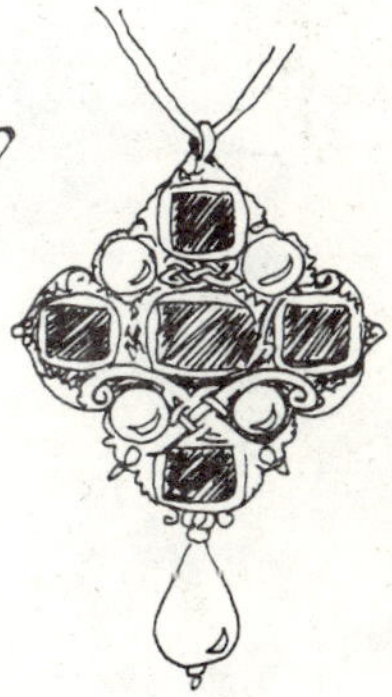

LADY ELIZABETH, HER GRACE, 1546

Early Tudor Female Costume

The early Tudor period in England (1500-1545), the age of the New Learning or the English Renaissance, was one of the most colorful, vigorous and creative eras of English history, setting the stage for the full flowering of the Elizabethan Age which followed. Like the Renaissance elsewhere, it marked the end of tradition in many areas, but more so in England than almost anywhere except Italy, for England lost many of its noble families in the Wars of the Roses and even its Plantagenet dynasty, which had ruled since 1066. The new ruling family, the Tudors, were descended from the Beaufort bastards of John of Gaunt and from a union between Henry V's widow and an insignificant Welshman named Owen Tudor. The Tudors were "new men" themselves and they attracted men like Wolsey and Cromwell who rose by ability, not by blood. Women, also, assumed a new role. Many medieval ladies had been active and effective in practical matters of ruling and as patrons of the arts. But for the first time, a whole generation of upper and middle class Tudor women were encouraged to equal their male counterparts in learning, and to use this knowledge to write and compose on their own. Although many prejudices remained, women of Tudor England came closer to intellectual and social equality than ever again for centuries.

Phyllis Cunnington writes: "Though to us the Tudor fashions seem to savor of fancy dress, their spirit was in fact far from fanciful. Rather were they portraits realistic of a full blooded generation with a background of brute force".[1] Tudor style was at the opposite extreme from the whimsical, sinuous, delicate decadence of the preceeding Gothic. It was aggressive, positive, even pushy, with the emphatic awkwardness of the new rich.

Full fashionable women's dress at this time consisted of (from the inside out) a shift or chemise, a corset, a farthingale, one or more petticoats, a kirtle and sometimes a gown.

The shift was of white thin linen, fitting closely the bodice, with a fairly full but not bulky skirt. The neckline was sometimes high and sometimes low and square, following the line of the kirtle bodice. The sleeves were very full, pleated into the arm-hole and closed with a drawstring into a full ruffle at the wrist. The shift was usually decorated at neck and wrists with a type of embroidery called blackwork or Spanish work, most commonly in black silk thread, but sometimes in gold or red. Some blackwork designs were geometric or related to the scrolling floral style of the previous century, but many designs were brought in by the Welsh Tudors from origins in Celtic interlace patterns.

Blackwork Designs

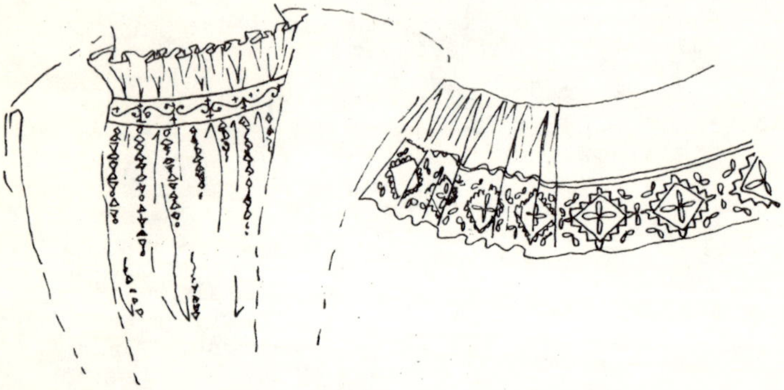

This embroidery was worked in line, stroke, or double running (Holbein) stitch. Holbein stitch can be found in most stitch directories. Any simple line stitch such as split stitch, back-stitch or outline stitch can also be used.

Either over or under the chemise was the corset. Its aim at this period was not so much to compress the waist (although it did to some extent) as to raise the bustline as high as possible and create an absolutely smooth, rigid triangle shape down to the waist. A modern longline strapless corset ("Merry Widow"), found in specialty corsetry shops, can easily be adapted by those who wish to cheat. Simply turn down the bra cups halfway and sew in place, so that the bust is pushed up to bulge over the top of the corset and is flattened beneath. The line of the corset top should just cover the nipples, no higher. If you are making a low-necked gown, the neckline should run exactly along the top edge of the corset.

If you wish to make your own corset, you will need a number of strips of slightly flexible but fairly rigid material such as thin metal, imitation whalebone (the stuff used in boned bras), thin wood, heavy leather, and so on. Make sure they are not too bulky, since the bodice of the dress must look smooth over the corset. Take your bust and waist measurement and reduce the waist about one inch if you wish. Robert Sartor describes the process of drafting the corset pattern as follows: "The waistline of the front piece is this measurement plus $\frac{1}{2}$ inch, while the waist on the back piece is this minus $\frac{1}{2}$ inch. This difference makes up for the back being narrower than the stomach".

Make the front and back curve down slightly from the center front to the underarm and up from the waistline over the hip bone. You can sew pockets for the individual strips of rigid material like Elizabethan "busks"), especially if they are metal, wood, or leather which you will want to remove for washing. The panels with these strips should be covered with one layer of cloth for lining and one on the outside for strength and a smooth line, and the whole should lace or hook at the center back.

Quarter of Corset Pattern

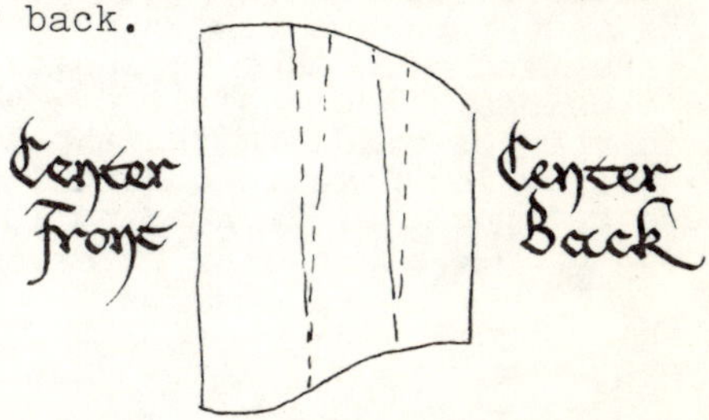

Another method is to use three or four panels of sturdy leather, pierced for ventilation and moulded while wet to a dress form. These are very much like the leather cuirasses worn by some fighters, and will produce a wide "cinch belt" laced together edge to edge at the sides and back center. The leather can be left plain or covered with cloth. The cloth will make it less sticky feeling in warmer weather.

At this point in dressing, the Tudor lady put on her stockings. Tudor stockings were knit. The first specific references to knitting occur at this time in England, although some authorities believe the craft existed much earlier. This is quite a controversial subject, however. Like all medieval women's hose, they reached only to the knee or just above and were tied or gartered there. Heavy dark or red knee-high hose are good approximations of Tudor stockings. (If you want to be absolutely authentic, you will want to remember that women, unlike men, wore no braes or underpants).

Over the corset went the farthingale or hoop skirt. This was of two types, the one of the early period being triangular was of two types, the one of the early period being triangular from waist to ground like a giant funnel, and the Elizabethan one being drum shaped. The funnel or Spanish style is far more attractive, and easier to make as well. For a small, easily handled farthingale about ten feet around at the hem, you will need three pieces of fourty-five inch material cut in triangles like side gores for a dress. Cut these full width at the base, narrowing to fit your waist at the top. The length, of course, will depend on your height.

Sew the farthingale just like a long skirt with a length of one hem left open and a waistband added, so that you can get it off and on, and close it with hooks and eyes at the waist. Hooks and eyes were now in use by the upper classes, and sometimes replaced lacing for invisible closings. Add a strip of material at the bottom hem, sewn along the two long edges like a the hoop which gives the farthingale its shape. Add these rod pockets, decreasing in length to form the fennel shape, at regular intervals of about a foot or

From Bellerphon Books

The corset, shift and Farthingale

eighteen inches, from the bottom hem to about mid-thigh. Cut a length of flexible tubing or imitation whalebone to fit each pocket and insert it like a cafe curtain rod into the pocket. Be sure the hoop end cannot escape. I discovered that, since I could not find a source of imitation whalebone, three-quarter inch aluminum tubing from the hardware store was light, cheap, and effective.

Over the farthingale you can put another petticoat if you wish. The petticoat is made exactly like the farthingale except without hoops: a simple full-length skirt.

At this point the Tudor lady added the first garment (except the neck and wrists of the shift) which was visible to the outside world, either the underskirt or the kirtle proper. With the Spanish farthingale the front of the overskirt was often opened from waist to hem in a wide inverted "V" shape, showing an underskirt of some rich fabric. This was often patterned if the overdress was plain or vice versa.

Popular fabrics for the underskirt were silk, brocades, cut or patterned velvet, satin, and cloth of gold. The satins of this period were usually still dull-faced ("antique satin"), although by the Elizabethan era mirror satin (bridal satin) had come into vogue. Tudor patterns were large scale and usually based on geometric or vegetable motifs. The stylized pomegranate design often found in drapery fabric is an authentic Tudor survival; Catherine of Aragon's personal badge was a pomegranate. Many of the traditional drapery patterns are Tudor in style, but be careful to avoid one of the Louis XVI and VI designs which are also common. After looking at several pictures from the two periods the difference will be instantly obvious. Tudor styles are heavy, solid, and rather rigid, while eighteenth century designs are light, flowing, and feminine in feeling. The false undersleeves usually match the underskirt, and the two will require about four or five yards for the underskirt and one yard for each undersleeve. The underskirt is again made in the same way as the farthingale and petticoat.

Since at least two whole books have been written about early Tudor costume, I can obviously only touch the surface of the topic. I will therefore deal only with the style of the time of Queen Anne (ca. 1530).

Some dresses of this period were high-necked with an open V-shaped collar and full but closed sleeves to the wrist. This style was more popular at a later time, during the reign of Mary and Edward. Most kirtles were cut quite low and square in the neck in front, with a sort of waist-length V-shape in the back. The bodice was plain and smooth with a round or slightly point waist. The point of the waist gradually increased until it reached the wasp-waisted effect of the Elizabethan age. The skirt could be full, closed in front, and gathered at the back of the waist, with a train.

High Necked kirtle with a French Hood

after Cunningham

If it was open in the front in the ∧shape, the skirt would be smooth, without any gathers, an ground length, usually without a train. The whole kirtle was of substantial material and fully lined to create a smooth architectural effect which did not reflect the shape of the body. The pattern which I used for this tyle was Butterick 4250, which is virtually an exact duplicate of the cutting diagram in Hill and Bucknell's <u>The Evolution of Fashion</u> for 1530.

The sleeves were tight at the armhole then widened into huge bell shapes and turned back about half way up the forearm. They were pinned around the upper arm to fall in a deep oval behind the elbow. The sleeve was lined with a contrasting fabric of fur. Underneath was a false sleeve which was tied or hooked into the upper sleeve just above the elbow. These false sleeves were cut in a semi-circle with a double layer of cloth interlined with very stiff stuff such as buckram to form a rigid cone or half circle shape. The interlining was often stuffed with hair, cotton, or some other material to make it rigid ("bombasted"). The back seam was often left open and held together at intervals with small jewelled broaches or clasps, and the shift sleeve was pulled out to puff between the clasps. The puffs and slashes were frequently carried around the whole wrist end of the false sleeve as a decoration. Over this outfit there was occasionally worn a loose A-line robe open in front called the gown, but this was rather rare in England. One of Henry the Eighth's later portraits also shows him wearing the masculine equivalent of the gown, a long, caftan-like garment.

Trained Kirtle Showing Front and Back Views after Cunningham

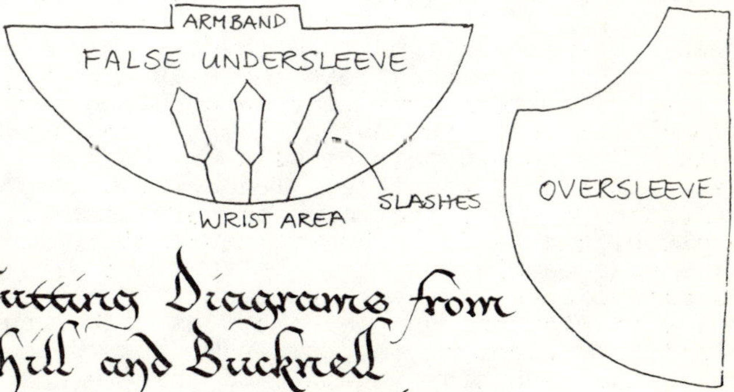

Cutting Diagrams from Hill and Bucknell

By far the most popular fabric in the early Tudor period was velvet, which was then a fairly stiff cloth with a low nap like velveteen. Other common fabrics included those used for underskirts as well: brocade, silk, damask, samite, satin, taffeta (then a rich, heavy cloth not at all like modern taffeta) and cloth of gold or silver, which actually had a warp and/or woof of metal beaten thin, drawn into fine wire and wrapped around silk thread or used alone. The Elizabethan period used many light pastel colors, but early Tudor favored rich, dark, jewel-like tones of black, red, gold, green, bronze, grey, or brown. Blue and tawney were used for servants and were usually avoided for noble garb. White accents were provided by the shift neckline, sleeve ruffle, and puffing. In addition to embroidery and cut or drawn work (a sort of primative lace), decorations included "guards", braid (called lace), and slashes or small cuts called pinking set in patterns, and geometric bands of goldsmith's work. The pinking, however, was more popular in men's clothing than in women's.

The accessories which were worn with this style included gloves, earrings, rings, and a kind of necklace which was wound around the neck like a choker, twisted in back and let fall down to disappear into the bodice. At the neck part of the necklace there was often a large pendant, and a matching pin was often placed at the center front of the bodice. Around the waist was a girdle made of cloth or metal with a single long piece falling down the center of the front and ending in a pomander, purse, book, rosary, dagger, or some other decorative article.

Shoes were flat with wide square toes, and were made of cloth, velvet, or leather. They covered the toes and were either simply slipped on like bedroom slippers or cut out in a square over the top of the foot and fastened with a strap. If you can find them regular slippers or flats with square toes like those used in Tai Chi (a form of martial arts) may be used. Otherwise you can make your own out of leather and heavy cloth. Use an old pair of slippers, taken apart, for a pattern if possible. Trace the sole or the bottom of your foot once on soft leather, once on cloth, and twice on heavy interfacing, then add a wide seam allowance. Do the same with the two side pieces, tracing two each of cloth and lining fabric, and shaping the toes either square or slightly wider at the toe end. Sew the two pieces for each side together on three sides,

Tudor Shoes

after Cunningham

leaving the sole edge open, and turn them right side out like a cuff or facing to make a finished edge at the ankle and the edges of the square cut out, if you add it. Sew these two finished side pieces together down the center front and back. Leave a part of the center front seam open, if you do not cut out the top, so that you can get it on your foot. Then add the ankle strap or a fastening at the center.

Next sew the four sole pieces together in a sandwich of cloth, interfacing, interfacing, and leather. Turn the finished set of side pieces inside out and sew them around the sole pieces so that the lining fabrics of both are together. Then turn the whole right side out. You should now have a slipper with a leather sole on the bottom, a lining, and an outside of velvet or cloth. The stiff material of the sole and sides of these shoes does not give a lot, which is why you need a wide seam allowance for sewing them together.

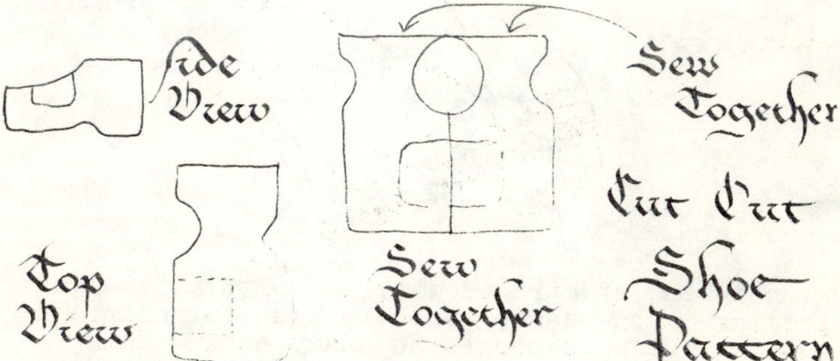

Shoe Pattern

Headgear for this style of garb was elaborate and is often the most difficult part of the costume to reproduce. Hair was parted in the middle and drawn back smoothly to be hidden under the hood. The three main kinds of headdress were caps like those of the men worn over an undercap, the French Hood and the Gable.

The early gable reached down past the shoulder in front, but by 1530 the sides had shortened to the jawline in front and been turned up at the sides. Underneath the whole thing was a white linen cap like a baby bonnet which tied under the chin, to which the hood was anchored with pins. This under-cap can be made by enlarging the bonnet pattern of a layette set, or by making a horseshoe-shaped back piece to fit your head and pleating into it a rectangular piece of material, then adding strings under the chin to tie it. Over this was

English Hood

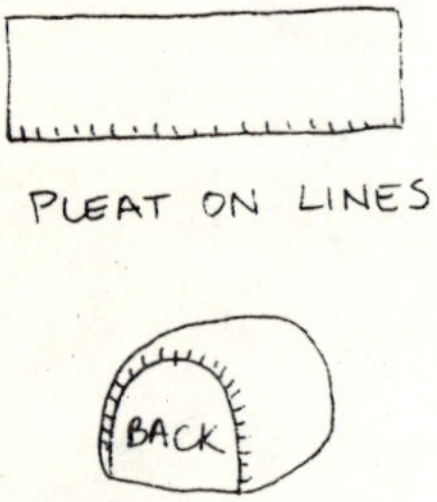

Cap Pattern

worn a band of striped material with a layer of padding in the center used to hide the hair and cushion the head under the heavy hood. This padded roll was wound around the head so that the center back rested on the nape of the neck and the two ends crossed over each other at the center front to be pinned to the cap.

The gable hood consisted of stiff back piece shaped like a diamond, a set of side pieces, a stiffened front gable with a band of metal or jewelry, and lappets which are turned up at the sides. The side and back pieces should be made of buckram, the very heavy interfacing used in hats and bridal headpieces, and covered with fabric. Along the edges between the buckram and the fabric, you should whipstitch a line of milliners' wire or any thin wire to hold their shape. You could also put a layer of cardboard between the buckram and cloth to stiffen it more. Notice that the bottom of the side pieces curves out away from the cheek. The front piece marked "gable" in the fig. below is a rigid piece of metal or wood covered with a jewelled band of trim. Sew the back piece together and add the side pieces and the gable, joining them edge to edge. The line marked "fold" on the center of the side piece joins at the point on the gable where it turns down against the cheek. The point marked "X" on the back and on the sides should meet. The lappets are cut in the same shape as the side pieces, and sewn so that both sides of the piece, top and bottom, are the right side of the material, because the bottom of the lappets will be turned back on the sides. The lappets are sewn to the side pieces down to the point just above where the side curves out from the cheek. The long rectangular piece at the

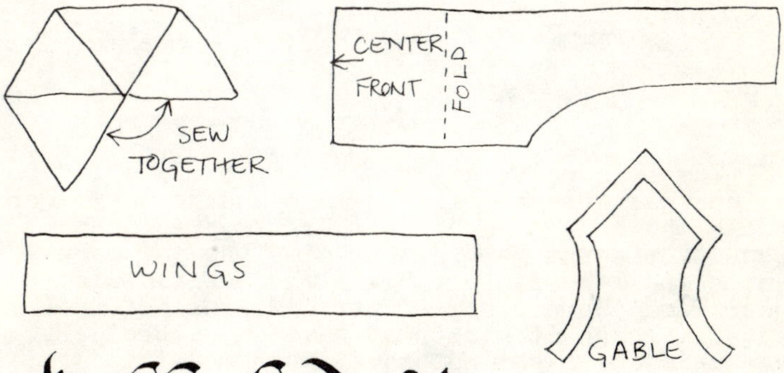

Gable Hood Pattern

end of the side piece should be extended to almost twice the length in the lappet as it is in the side piece. When the sides and lappet are sewn together, the end of the lappet which hangs down beyond the bottom of the side piece is turned back up and pinned to the top of the hood (see fig. below). Leave the edge of the lappet which fits against the bottom angle of the back piece open and sew the "wings" to the underlying side piece of the hood, then sew down the lappet material to give a nice finished edge. The wings were usually of black velvet, interliner, and were sewn in at about a fourty-five degree angle at the bottom of the hood back to hang down beyond the waist in back. For their placement, see the back of fig. on pg. 126. To finish the hood, cut out a shape of some contrasting material and sew it in over the sides and back as a lining.

Since there has been an article on constructing a French Hood published in Tournaments Illuminated, I will not include any such instructions here. The French Hood is the rigid semicircular headdress familiar to us from portraits of Anne Boleyn and Katherine Howard, one of whose portraits is the basis for fig. on pg. 125

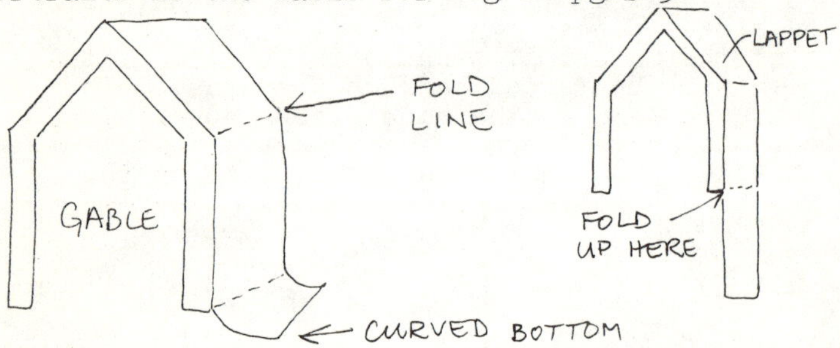

There is no question that upper class Tudor costume was a royal pain to make and to wear. For people who cannot face the thought of so much trouble, peasant garb at the time was far more simple and more comfortable. The lower class Tudor woman wore a shift just like that of the lady, although it might not have any embroidery. Over this she might not have another petticoat, because the back of the kirtle was sometimes caught up in the center back of the girdle to keep it out of the dirt and make movement easier. But the peasant probably would not have a corset, false sleeves, or a farthingale. Her kirtle would lace down the center front to about the waist, and have plain straight sleeves like those of a caftan. She often wore a long apron over the kirtle skirt.

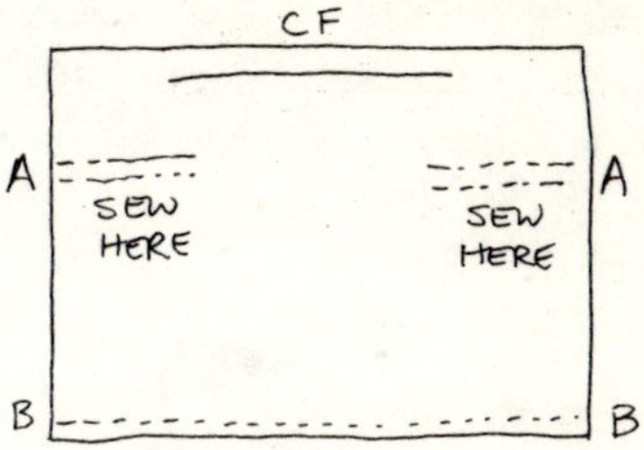

Peasant clothes were made of a coarse homespun material of wool, linen or a mixture of the two. Natural colors like green and brown ("russet") were the most common. Stockings were cloth, not knit, and many cheap furs and skins were used, such as cat or rabbit.

Lower class headdresses were also much simpler. The undercap might be worn alone, or a length of plain rectangular cloth over the head like a medieval headrail. One type of simple cap was the peasant version of the French Hood, which, was similar to the figure above. This headdress is made from two plain rectangles of heavy white cloth about twenty-five by twenty inches. The front edge is wired from ear to ear length. The two rectangles are sewn together on three sides, and the open edges hemmed. The lines marked"sew here" on fig. above are sewn on this wrong side. The whole is then turned right side out. The two front lappets thus created are pinned up on the side of the cheek, as shown above, and the back section AA-BB is sewn together at the edges to make a wide tube which encloses the hair. Two ribbons are sewn to the inside front at about the level of the cheekbones, and are tied under the chin.

And now you have seen how to make Tudor costume-

aren't you glad you're a Norman!

BIBLIOGRAPHY

Cunnington and Cunnington. Handbook of English Costume in the XVI Century.

Hill and Bucknell. The Evolution of Fashion.

Henry VIII & His Wives. Bellerophon Books.

Herbert Norris. Costume and Fashion. Volume III, Book I.

Private letter from Robert Trump (Robert Sartor).

after a Painting by Frederigo Zuccaro

Mary, Queen of Scots

Anne of Cleves

after a Painting by Cranach, c. 1526

from Francesco Cossa's
Allegory for April

A Note on Italian Renaissance Garb

Renaissance, of course, is a difficult term to define, and different authorities argue endlessly about just what it means. In general, however, we can date the Renaissance in Italy as beginning in the thirteenth century, the era of Dante, and reaching its high point in the fifteenth century. The Italian influence spread slowly outward, reaching France and England in the early sixteenth century and extending to Russia at last in the time of Peter the Great. Along with works of art and ideas of humanism went details of costume. This was significant since Italy had a distinctive style of its own, although it, of course, echoed the general tendencies of the age. In part this was because it was one of the most cosmopolitan areas of the western world, trading with Byzantium and the Arab world, and, through them, with the Far East.

In many cases, garments pictured in Italian sources do not differ greatly from those found in other areas, especially in the early period. This may be either because Italy shared in the general clothing styles of the west (e.g. Dante is always shown in the same long, loose thirteenth-century robe seen all over Europe at that time), or because Italian styles were exported to other areas. Much of early sixteenth century male garb is highly Italian in inspiration, and it would be a bit redundant to describe in detail all aspects of male garb, when many are already treated in the section on sixteenth century Tudor costume.

The short pourpoint or doublet worn over a full shirt and laced to waist-length hosen ("tights"), as described in the Male Tudor, was the most common Italian style. This was sometimes worn alone, but frequently a short over-garment was worn, shaped like a tabard with loose or formal pleats across the entire front width. The sides were open; the neck might be straight across in a horizontal opening, showing [illegible] tabard was simply two lengths of fabric sewn together at one end, or it might form a slight V shape in front. This tabard might be belted all the way around the waist, around the front only (leaving the back section free) or entirely unbelted. Even small children are pictured in this universal style. Sometimes this outer garment was converted into a tunic by adding sleeves, either closed or open from the shoulder in "wings". The result was very close to the fashionable short tunic with puffed sleeves and pleated front found in England during the high Gothic period, the reign of Edward IV. This style is copiously illustrated. One example, from the Medici palace in Florence shows both sleeved and sleeveless styles. Lorenzo de Medici is also shown in this picture wearing an interesting costume which is shaped like a cotehardie down to the hips, with a wide gold belt there, and underneath a bases skirt. The sleeves are open fron the elbow. Beneath this he wears a tunic with a high collar and

Lorenzo de Medici c.1459

and plain tight sleeves to the wrist. The date for this picture is 1459. It is an unusual design which may be explained since it was intended to be worn as garb for an "oriental fete". Next to Lorenzo's horse is a young man with a tunic of one fabric and full sleeves puffed on the shoulder but tight on the forearm in another material. The skirt of the tunic is full and is belted into many folds. The chest is not pleated, but other figures in the picture show the pleated style of this tunic as well. The mounted figure near Lorenzo is wearing the style with the open tabard. This one picture therefore shows the two styles most closely associated with the Renaissance. Heads were often left bare, especially by young men, who laid great stress on their beautiful hair. The shoulder-length, smooth "pageboy" style was the most common hairstyle. Sometimes a hat was worn; two styles which appear in the picture are the flat beaver hat described at the beginning of the Male Tudor and a hat shaped like a fez with an upturned brim. All the examples of the latter are in red in this picture.

Many of the male Italian fashions emigrated and appeared in other areas of Europe some years after they were fashionable in their homeland. For example, cutte hosen and the sleeve puffed at the shoulder (mentioned above) and the tubular sleeve divided into two pieces at the elbow took some twenty years or more to work their way north to England. The V-shaped front of the pourpoint laced over a plackard and the simar long gown worn over it were typical of Italian style, as was the netted undercap. Bases, the pleated military skirt, originated in Italy in the late fifteenth century. An example of the local way of wearing them is shown here. Note the imaginative hat (a type of Milan bonet), characteristic of the more light-hearted fashions popular in Italy. Many of these fanciful hats seem to have been influenced by the classical revival associated with the Renaissance, which made fancy-dress balls popular at that time and led to recreations of pseudo-classical costumes.

For unknown reasons, female costume did not travel as readily as male garb, and women's dress remained more distinctively Italian than male. One characteristic frequently seen was the low round (rarely square) neckline with the very high Empire waist. The upper bodice might be of the same fabric or the fabric of the skirt, but was often a different material and richly decorated with jewels or trim. The sleeves might be of the same fabric or the fabric of the skirt. The effect created was of a short jacket like the "Spencer" of the French Empire period over a long, long,

Italian
1510-20

flowing skirt. The sleeves were the most elaborated part of the costume, often divided, slashed, puffed, or otherwise decorated. A good example of this style can be seen in a picture by Carpaccio of two Venetian cortesans. It was a fashion popular especially in Florence to wear the high-waisted gown, sometimes with a tabard-like panel in front and back flowing freely, and with long, open oversleeves falling like "wings" from the shoulder to the floor.

Italian women's dress was generally simpler and more flowing than that of the northern countries. The fantastic slashing and bombasting was never much used and the farthingale was unpopular. The "Italian sleeve" was like that of the men, and the name was given generally to any style divided into two parts with the undergarment puffing out through the divisions. A more elaborate version can be seen following, taken from a picture of the Empress Eleanor of Portugal in a fresco in the library at Siena. A portrait of the Princess Mary of England from about 1520 (this being Henry VIII's sister, not his daughter) attributed to Jan van Mabuse, shows a typical northern adaptation of Italian styles. The neckline is cut square in the style used on English costume, but not as wide or low as the fashionable English neckline worn with the farthingale. The bodice is also flat and waist-length, rather than Empire-waisted. However, the Italian influence shows in the diamond design used to decorate the front of the bodice, in the Italian divided sleeve also decorated with the diamond pattern, and in the flowing skirt of narrow panels of silver tissue bordered with gold cords, worn without the farthingale. The lady also wears an Italian headdress of a style which will be described below.

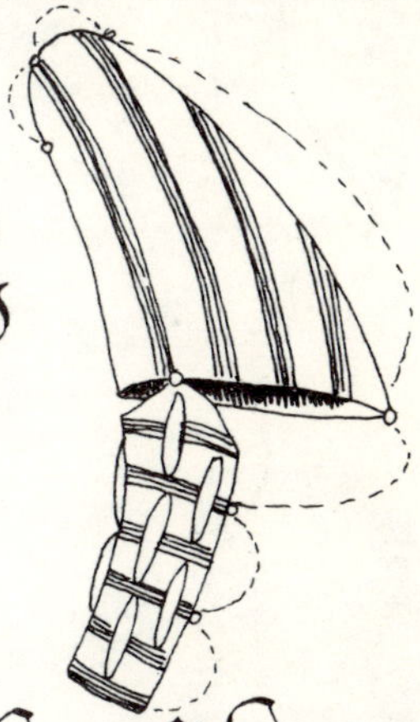

Italian women's headdress was highly distinctive. Elaborate headdresses were not popular even during the fifteenth century, although examples can be seen in contemporary paintings of ladies wearing the heart-shaped headdress. Instead, fanciful designs in real and false hair were favored. The hair was puffed, frizzled, braided, twisted, and shaped in an amazing variety of ways, often decorated with feathers, jewels, and ropes of pearls in many fantastic designs. One example from a wealth of individualistic designs is found in the portrait of Simonetta Vespucci painted by Botticelli, which can be seen on the next page. (this by the way, was the lady better known as the "Venus on the half shell" from the "Birth of Venus").

When headdresses were worn, they were usually simple. Wreaths of fresh flowers were not uncommon. Most permanent styles were based on networks of heavy cords. A basic kind of net headdress appears in a portrait of Beatrice d'Este by Leonardo da Vinci from the early sixteenth century. It is a

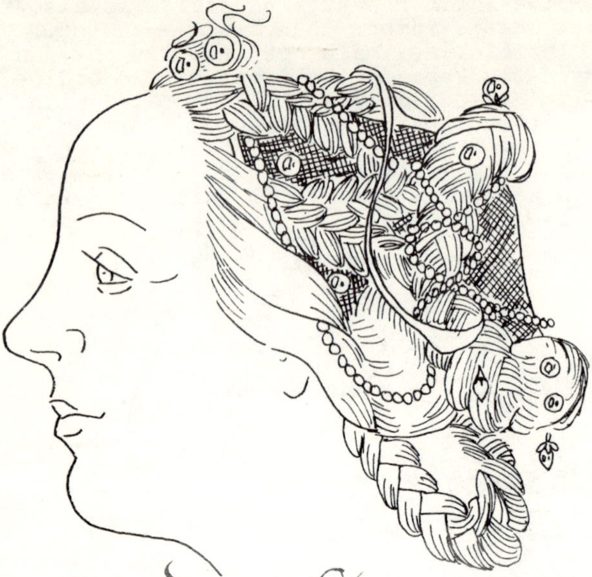

net square set well back on the head, prevented from slipping off by a fillet bound around the lady's forehead. Another style from the same period was to cover the top of the head with a net caul of gold and pearls, then the long hair is divided into two sections which are not braided, but are bound at intervals by a ribbon would around each one, like the stripes around a barber-shop pole or on a candy cane. The two length of hair are then brought around the head, being crossed at the nape of the neck, and the ends tucked in underneath at the forehead. This gives the effect of a roll of hair, widest at the nape and narrow at the forehead, surrounding the whole head like a halo, with the top of the head filled in by a network of gold cord.

Unshaped veils were still worn in Italy long after they had gone out of fashion elsewhere. They were sometimes placed on the back of the head in the same position as the net square and held in place with a fillet in the same way, but they were also worn in the normal "madonna" fashion over the entire head. Another Italian style, adopted by the Spanish, was the reticulated caul. This was another type of net headdress; in this one a long tube of net was suspended from the

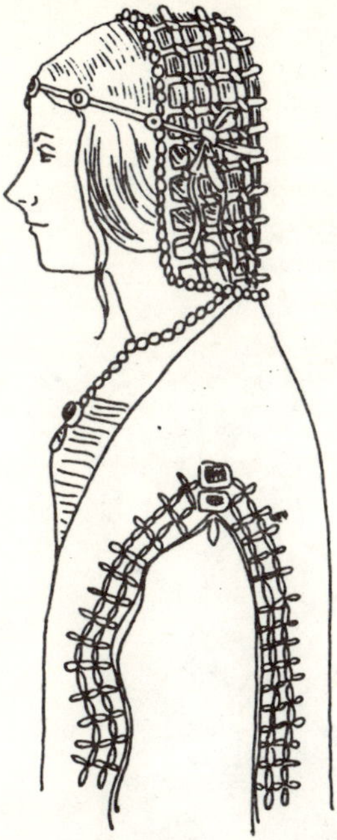

after a painting of Beatrice d'Este by Leonardo da Vinci showing a netted hairstyle

back of the head and stuffed with hair. Since the network tube often reached to the feet, false hair was obviously added. The whole looked like a long plait of hair encased in a small round tube, almost exactly like the casings for braids worn during the Norman period, except that this style was in one piece of hair and fell down the back. The network casing was criss-crossed with ribbons and decorated with an ornament at the end.

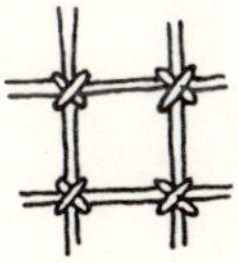

Details of net and jewels

after a Woodcarving by Peter Dell
c. 1530 Allegory of Lust

Sex and the Single Surcoat

or

Effects of Population Pressure on Clothing Styles in England in the Thirteenth Through Sixteenth Centuries

It is a common observation that a person's clothes reflect his psychology or "self-image", sometimes consciously and sometimes not. It is also obvious that the message one culture gets from a style of garb often differs widely from that of another culture. Bare breasts are shocking today, while an Elizabethan would be more likely to react to unbound hair, and a Victorian could wax lustful (if we are to believe the writings of the time) over an unclothed leg of lamb or a naked table limb. It is, therefore, a risky proposition, if not a sign of incipient hubris, to try to deduce the psychological meaning of a country's high-style in clothing over a period of centuries. Nevertheless, the author is about to attempt this feat, all the while crossing her fingers and trying to dodge the rotten tomatoes from the audience.

The thirteenth century was the Medieval Century in England par excellence. Feudalism was at its height, with all land in effect involved in the seignorial chain of ownership, with an as yet very limited influence by the merchants and free towns outside the system. Absent, weak or unpopular kings like Richard, John and Henry III allowed much of the government to pass from the king into the hands of the great feudal lords. The so-called Renaissance of the Twelfth Century, which had resulted from the reception of classical literature from Byzantium (along with Arabic commentary), was becoming systemized and frozen into a form of orthodoxy by such thinkers as Thomas Aquinas. The process was, of course, a long and complicated one, and it took many years before Aquinas's conclusions were accepted generally. However, his work is a good example of the thirteenth century impulse to chase down every independent concept or "authority" and cram it into a general system of accepted philosophy. The great spiritual upheavals which had produced new monastic movements like the Franciscans, the Dominicans and the Carthusians, calling for personal examination and purification of the Church, became institutionalized into established orders and lost their fierce individual drive. There was much private violence, but the population was relatively high and pressed upon the resources of the land. The previous century had seen a lot of land reclamation in the waste areas, particularly by these very monastic houses, and much of the usable land was now occupied, or at least claimed.

All these influences produced an atmosphere of conformity. Each person saw himself less as an individual than as a member of a group: a link in a family chain from father to son, a lord's "man", a member of a religious order or guild, one of the serfs belonging to some fief. Thirteenth century dress is generally considered one of the simplest and least decorated styles in all medieval history. The design was essentially unisex, the only major difference being the length of the skirt and the headdress. Styles avoid the shape of the body, although in a far more natural manner than those of the sixteenth century. The tunics, robes, guard-corps and sideless surcoats covered their wearers in a neat, dignified and modest manner, concealing sex and identity. There is very little trim or decoration, and the only outlet for display is in the quality of the cloth itself. With the advent of the cyclas, which had at first been designed to cover a lord's armor and help identify him in battle, display of heraldic arms on male and female garments became popular. Thus the wearer was merged completely with his armorial identity as an heir of his family.

Thirteenth century garb was practical and comfortable, and has demonstrated its usefulness in monastic habits ever since. It has no exaggerated features, and is essentially a sensible costume, warm in winter under a pelicon (a loose furlined robe), cool in summer in a light fabric, and protected from the weather by sturdy cloaks, caps, hoods and voluminous but simple veils and wimples. But many of the garments, especially the women's and monastic ones, the only parts of the body visible were the face and hands. Everything else was not only decently covered by completely obscured by billowing, ungirdled volumes of cloth.

Toward the middle of the fourteenth century, the psychological climate in England began to change. The advent of more forceful, charismatic rule under the Edwards made the king a more personally compelling figure. The centralizing tendency thus begun continued with brief setbacks under Richard II and Henry VI right into the Renaissance New Monarchy of the Tudors. The Hundred Years War with France began about 1350, and it provided another centralizing patriotic force, since the war was generally popular, although the limited nature of medieval warfare did not involve large numbers of people. However, the war provided a steady drain on the population, and to add to this in 1348 came the first visitation of the Black Plague. This dread disease, which recurred periodically thereafter, had an overwhelming effect. The first few attacks were naturally the worst, wiping out half the population generally, and sometimes almost one hundred percent in smaller areas.

These influences reduced the numbers of people suddenly and drastically, and brought about a new concept of death. Death, even sudden, violent death, had always been familiar to the medieval world, but such wholesale and meaningless mortality created a new sense of the precariousness of life. This resulted in the usual reactions, either a deeper personal concern for religion and one's spiritual state, or a hedonistic determination to enjoy the moment.

All at once, the individual became more important. As the number of peasants shrank, each laborer acquired greater leverage toward easing feudal burdens or demanding higher wages. The end result of this movement was the Peasants' Revolt which was put down under Richard II, and a continuing discontent which smoldered for generations. At the other end of the social scale, what wealth there was in the noble class contracted into fewer hands. Money had become more and more important in the economy, which was moving away from feudal self-sufficiency and payment in kind. Those of the nobility (and, increasingly, the rich merchant class) who had good incomes had their resources not in grain and cattle, but in cash which could be saved up and exchanged for foreign goods like rare cloth. With the growing number of absentee lords who left their fiefs to their bailiffs to follow the court or live in town, and with the growing number or rich guildsmen who did not wish to invest their surplus in land, display in clothing became a favorite way of gaining and showing status.

Dress reflected these developments. The tight, low-necked coathardie became fashionable, form-fitting to the hips on both men and women, and, for men, quite short, sometimes revealing not only the thighs but even the genitals under the hosen. A wide jewelled belt was placed about the hips of both sexes to emphasize further the pelvic area. Women's hair was usually visible in braids, cauls, or templars. Such sexually explicit garb was an almost inevitable, but probably unconscious, response to the need for a higher birthrate to replace the plague deaths.

For the fashionable, the coathardie and its metallic belt were made of highly decorated, rich material, often heavily embroidered and bejewelled. Despite the small volume of fabric, the coathardie could be very expensive indeed, for it served as both display and a form of investment. Land was less valuable since much of it was unworkable due to lack of labor, and a part of the former cropland was enclosed for grazing sheep for the wool trade. Both these factors added to the growing money economy and to the use of non-perishable goods as investments for excess income. Oddly enough, jewelry for ears or neck was almost never worn in this period, probably because the focus of dress was so strongly in the hip area.

As the century wore on and moved into the fifteenth, the dreadful urgency to increase the population declined and the coathardie went out of fashion. Nevertheless, the pregnant look (rounded belly, high waistline, forward pelvic thrust) continued in most fifteenth century styles. Nor could the clock be turned back: the new awareness of the body and individuality remained. Conspicuous consumption reached its height in the houppeland, which was of rich material like the coathardie but with vastly greater yardage.

The lower classes in the fifteenth century resumed some of the growth and stability of the thirteenth, although the wars in France, the enclosure movement, peasant unrest and a growing money economy remained. For the noble class, however, the Wars of the Roses began around 1337 and continued with growing virulence until Bosworth Field at the end of the fifteenth century. The sense of one's place in an orderly pattern of history all but vanished, and the old families found relatives fighting each other and numbers much reduced. High Gothic dress had something in common with garb in late eighteenth century France (where social forces were similar): light, delicate patterns and colors in fabric; and fancifulness, extravagance and exaggeration in design.

Awareness of the body was more sophisticated. Skirts, while long and trailing, revealed the figure in front or were gathered up in a way suggesting fertility over the stomach. Main emphasis was shifted from the pelvic area to the breasts in the high-girdled, V-necked gown, which often was open to the waist in front and back. Face hair, foreheads and eyebrows were plucked, and perfume and cosmetics were popular with both men and women.

Many of the Gothic styles, even the more frivalous ones, were graceful and flowing, but there was a certain air of decadence about them. Mnay shapes were pointed and over-delicate: steeple henins, liripipes, piked shoes, pointed sleeves and trains, the sugarloaf hat and vertical lines of men's dress of about 1470. The look was attenuated as if to reflect the vanishing of the noble families. The amazing women's headdresses and the elaborately dagged and decorated men's garb showed imagination, playfulness and aristocratic taste, but a lack of common sense. It was a style divorced from practicality which clearly said, "Apres moi le deluge".

With the accession of Henry VII, there was an abrupt break in English history in many areas. The Tudors were an upstart dynasty, unsure of their lineage and hotly jealous of the few more direct survivors of the Plantagenets. They represented the New Monarchies movement in England, the establishment of an essentially non-feudal, fully centralized royal government, with a theoretical foundation of classical political theory. While the King has been reminded of his divinely appointed responsibilities for centuries, his "divine right" and absolute authority first became accepted doctrine in this period.

The population had become numerous again by this time and especially after the dissolution of the monasteries, there were large numbers of poor people and beggars without any means of support; i,e., more people than places or work for them.

Some of these were actually former religious, but there were also many boarders, lay workers, and charity cases which had depended on the monastic houses as well. A move toward urbanization was also well under way. In addition to the uprooting of traditional lifestyles and personal identities, this led to crowding in the cities and all the problems of crime, unemployment, housing, and so on that we are familiar with today. The old Mother Goose Rhyme "Hark, Hark, the dogs do bark; The beggars are coming to town", reflects this social unrest of the time and the dismay of the stable folk who saw themselves threatened.

The New Learning, as Renaissance Humanism was known in England, had become popular, questioning many traditional beliefs and attempting (to a degree) to force contemporary realities into a long-outmoded classiciam. Women and laymen were becoming prominent in scholarly fields on a large scale for the first time since ancient Rome. Not mere negative anti-clericalism but the positive secularism of the Italian Renaissance infused the education of the upper classes, while at the same time the partisan faiths of the Reformation demanded a personal commitment in religion.

It was an age of tremendous psychological insecurity. There was the social insecurity of a violently upwardly mobile age in which power and wealth were available to almost anyone with ability, ruthlessness, and drive. But the rise of a Wolsey or a Cromwell not only threatened the old nobility but prompted a burning discontented ambition in those who felt they had been unfairly passed over. This created a geninely Machiavellian atmosphere of pragmatism wherein loyalty, conscience, gentleness, good manners, personal dignity and aristocratic pride were lost in an all-consuming push to the top. There was the religious insecurity of the reformation, particularly in England where the issue of Protestant, Independent, Calvinist, and Catholic swayed back and forth through the reigns of Henry, Edward, Mary, Elizabeth, James, Charles I, Cromwell, and Charles II for over a hundred years, with each generation claiming victims from the presently unpopular viewpoints.

There was also a considerable sexual insecurity among the fashionable classes. The old role of the feudal nobility as warriors had been largely eliminated. Professionals and non-nobles more and more took over fighting for the king abroad, and the Tudors firmly checked any intra-feudal private battles at home. Except for a sturdy few like the percies on the northern marches, there was little way for noble lords to define their identity, and games like tournaments or infighting for the kings favor at court did not really satisfy their masculinity. At the same time, women of the upper classes were demanding more freedom and showing their competence in previously "male" areas. The Wars of the Roses had left many female heirs to old houses, and they were sometimes no longer content to be mere pawns in the hands of their distant male relatives. The strong women who had formerly been shunted into the nuneries and forgotten now remained in secular life to carve out a place in competition with men. Shakespeare's female characters, articulate, self-confident, able, and independent, show how far the concept of women's range had come from the passive heroines of medieval romances like Morte D'Arthur or Roman De La Rose. (Reality, of course, was always another matter; there were plenty of tough-minded, competent women in the Middle Ages). The entire situation had much in common with the psychological problems of today, with its conflicting ideologies and changing sex roles.

Among the ruling family, this sexual insecurity was intense. Henry VIII with his search for a wife to bear him a son, Mary the long-term spinster who never had a child but did have several hysterical pregnancies, Edward who died a boy, Elizabeth who gloried in the title "the Virgin Queen", and James, a homosexual: these were hardly sexual successes. Since royalty now dictated fashion, their personal hang-ups affected dress in general. It will also be remembered that, briefly, Mary, and then Elizabeth were the first reigning Queens of England since Anglo-Saxon times, and Elizabeth was they first successful Queen at all. That the people would accept them was, in itself, a sign of how far women had come: a long way, baby, indeed!

All these elements are faithfully reflected in the garb of the period. It has been described as "nouveau gauche": gaudy, awkward, and overdecorated, one of the most thoroughly unnatural styles ever created. A lack of spontaneity and whimsey was reflected in the dark emphatic colors (lightening in Elizabethan times), geometric shapes, and rigid patterns in fabric and jewelry. There was considerable opportunity for display, much of it ostentatious and vulgar, in the vast amounts of velvet, satin, brocade, cloth of gold, fur, and jewels required for high fashion in dress. As in earlier days, fine garb reflected new wealth, disguised the social upstart, and insinuated the insignificant into areas where he might be noticed. But unlike the Gothic period, many of the rich were not from the aristocratic tradition, their finery was artificial, based not on the good taste of the person within, but on the professional tailoring available without.

The Gothic awareness of the body had vanished, and the one within the garment had become totally irrelevant. Female dress was constructed in architectural fashion upon a rigid framework of corset, farthingale, and hood. Men's garb, with its wide shoulders during Henry's reign and the variety of shaping and bombastine throughout the period, was equally divorced from the human being underneath. More and more the pieces of the costume became separated from one another as well as from the wearer. There were huge puffed sleeves, wide skirts, men's padded slops which separated legs from trunk, and disembodied faces floated above the ruff like the head of John the Baptist on a platter. Decoration was added without concern for the function or total design, especially embroidery, jewels, and slashing.

The whole of sexual identity in Tudor clothing is either negative or confused. At first sight, the Henrician design with its bombasted shoulders and obviously <u>macho</u> codpiece looks quite masculine. But, while the coathardie expressed a genuine pride in the wearers' maleness, Henry's masculine attributes were exaggerated and artificial, tacked on by the tailor rather than revealed by the figure. This design showed the over-emphasis of the neurotic which was amply reflected in Henry's six marriages. Later male garb retreated completely from masculinity into foppish colors and styles, little pseudo-skirts of trunk hose and pansied slops, ruffs borrowed from female styles, and the strange false pregnancy of the peascod belly. (The use of the term "pansy" as an insulting term for male homosexuals has sometimes been linked to "pansied slops", as a matter of fact). It is little wonder that the pioneers who carved out homesteads in the New World and harried the Spanish Main adopted a much simpler style of dress away from court.

Women faired no better. Even during the Henrician period architectural hoods concealed the hair and rigid corsets flattened the breasts, while cone-shaped Spanish farthingales hid the shape of the lower body. With the Virgin Queen, all traces of fertility and function disappeared from women's dress. No matter whether the breasts were covered or visible in the low square neckline, the shape of the upper body was childlike, with a flattened bustline which denied the function of the breasts. The tightly corseted waist was gradually lowered and narrowed to eliminate the shape of the hips. The skirts spread out farther and farther, developing into the absurd drum farthingale. This contraption made the wearer look like a flattened triangle rising out of a round cage like a hatbox. With attack below denied by the farthingale and attack above warded off by the ballooning ruff and sleeves, the late Elizabethan woman seemed impregnable both figuratively and literally. The survival of the English upper classes must be attributed to the good sense of those members of it who ignored the message their garb (and Queen) intended.

A brief addendum: During the homosexual James's reign, men's clothing remained foppish and fantastic, while women's became tube-like and entirely shapeless. With the reign of Charles I, an eminently normal, happily married man, male garb became elegant, dignified, and attractively masculine, while women's clothing was modest and conducive to comfortable pregnancy.

It is almost impossible to prove a correlation between factors of population and styles of dress. Yet it is equally hard not to see a relationship. Styles change, often without any more conscious reason than boredom, but the direction in which they change reflects the general climate of society and the individual peculiarities of leading figures like royalty. Of course, high fashion always affects only a small minority who have the income and leisure to wear clothes for display rather than use. The clothing of the working people of Tudor England, for example, had only a distant similarity to the garb of the court. You could not milk a cow in a farthingale or mow a field in the peascod belly, yet the general atmosphere of over-population and insecurity certainly influenced both upper and lower classes. Thus, at the risk of considerable subjectivism, changing garb can provide an interesting, sometimes useful, tool in the analysis of changing cultures.

Cutting Patterns

ABOUT THE CUTTING DIAGRAMS

This section is to help a beginning costumer get started by suggesting what sort of mundane patterns might be altered to produce the basis of a period pattern. Be sure to refer back to the chapters that relate to the major styles illustrated by the following cutting diagrams. Each chapter gives specific information of what variations and accessories are appropriate for a complete costume. Other cutting diagrams that relate to the major styles are indexed for easier referral.

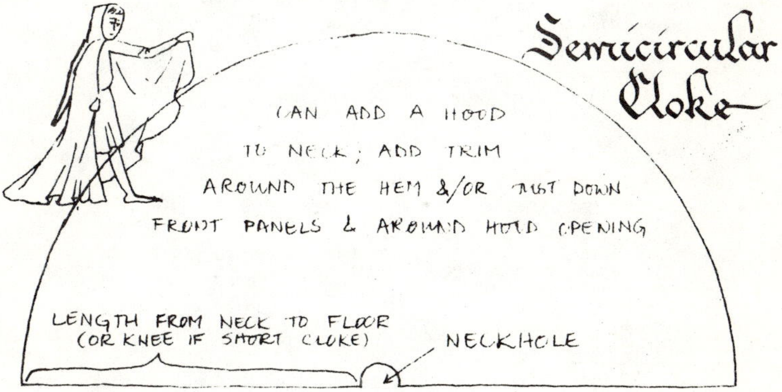

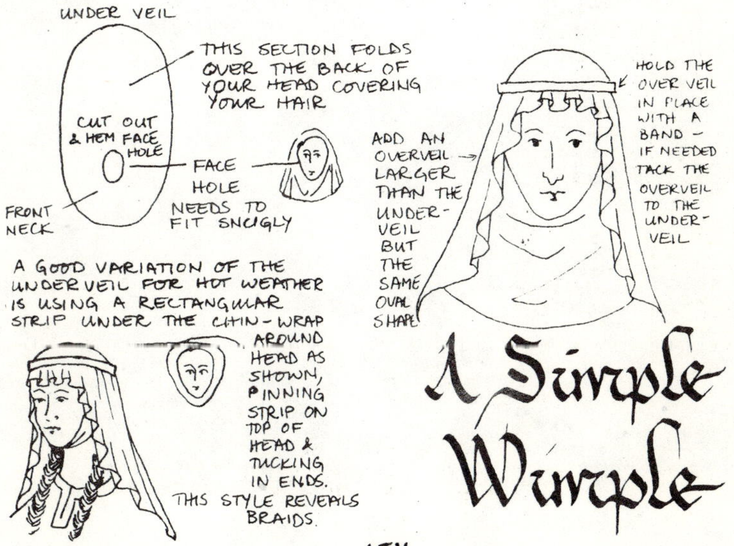

The Basic T-Tunic

All styles from Byzantine until the early fourteenth century can be constructed from the basic T-tunic cut, except the bliaut. You <u>should</u> know how to make a T-tunic by now. Once again, simply fold a length of material in half lengthwise (about four yards for floor length, two or three for shorter lengths), cut the desired neckline in the center of the folded end, and adapt the sleeves. Byzantine, Saxon, and early Norman are constructed in a straight T shape with a ninety degree angle at the underarm, as shown below. The style of around 1190 has a shallow curve under the arm, described in the chapter on that period. If the sleeve is not long enough to reach the wrist, which it probably won't be with any normal width of cloth, unless you are a midget, piece the ends of fabric. Period, you know.

Be sure to refer to the Chapters "Byzantines and Barbarians", "Costumes of the 12th and 13th centuries", and the first part of "The Wonderful 14th Century".

Additional Cutting Diagrams of interest:

p. 26 Dalmatica
p. 40 Saxon Tunic
p. 48 Cotte
p. 49 Bliant
p. 50 Funnel Hood
p. 56 Hood Cuts
p. 58 Oriental Surcote
p. 59 Cyclas
p. 61 Gardcorp, Coif
p. 66 Circular Cloke
p. 68 Chaperon

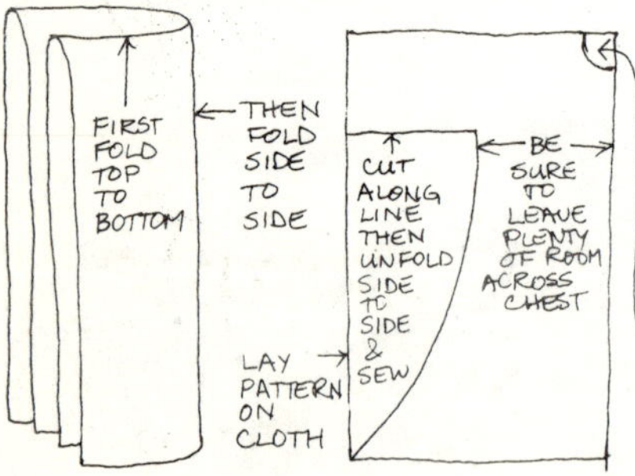

See these drawings of women's variations of the T-tunic.

p. 32 Byzantine
p. 37 Teutonic
p. 43 Capelet
p. 53 Norman Sleeves
p. 55 Women's Bliant
p. 64 Hairstyles besides the Simple Wimple

Cut of Teutonic Overtunic

SEE P. 37

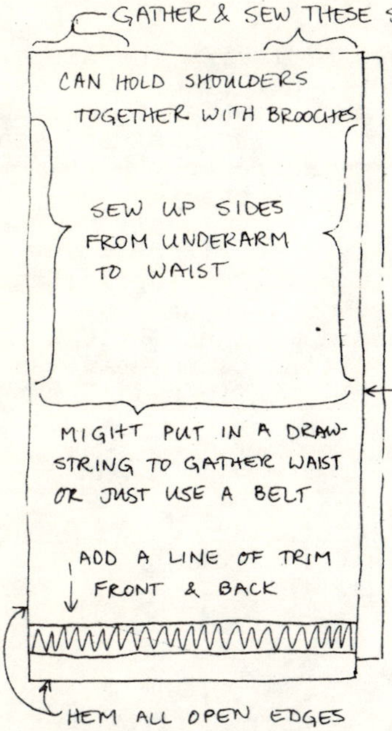

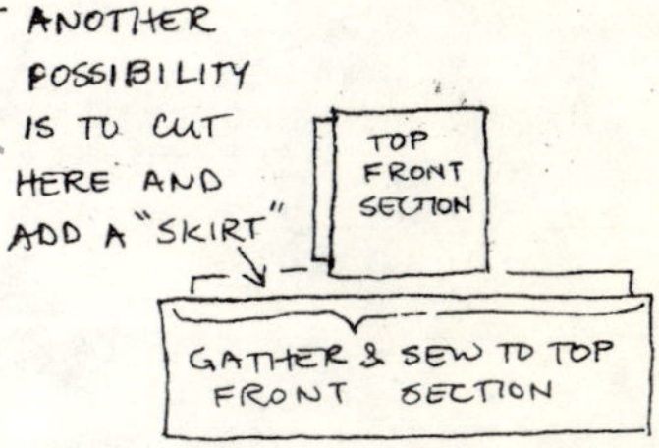

ALMOST ALL WOMEN'S STYLES, AND MANY MEN'S, REQUIRE AN UNDERTUNIC- USUALLY WITH LONG TIGHT SLEEVES- AND AN OVERTUNIC- USUALLY WITH A LOOSER SHORTER SLEEVE. THE OVERTUNIC IS EITHER SHORTER OR DRAWN UP TO SHOW THE TUNIC UNDERNEATH. THIS VERY SIMPLE GARB CAN BE VERY ELEGANT WITH SUMPTOUS EMBROIDRY AND FINE JEWELRY.

EMBROIDRY

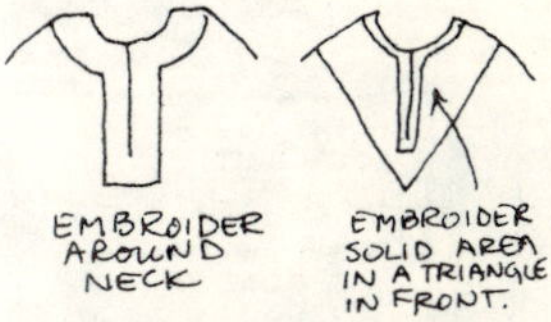

HEMS AROUND SLEEVES & SKIRT ARE GOOD PLACES FOR EMBROIDRY TOO.

FOR KNOTWORK, TRY A CHAIN-STITCH IN WOOL OR PAINT ON LIQUID EMBROIDRY & THEN OUTLINE WITH A BACKSTITCH IN EMBROIDRY FLOSS.

Lady's Cotehardie

For a lady's cotehardie, take any princess-style pattern with a round scooped neckline. Choose one cut in six pieces, since that was the way the original cotehardie excavated at Herjolssnes was cut.

Fit the bodice tightly, replacing the zipper with a line of lacing. Cut the neckline down to the depth you wish, depending on how fashionable you want to be. If you want, put the entire dress together and simply cut the neckline on the wearer, cutting off the tops of the sleeves at the shoulder and fitting the upper body closely to the owner. Widen the skirt panels from either waist or hip length to the full width of the fabric, and add gores if needed at the seams. Adjust the sleeves as necessary to make them tight throughout and add a placket with buttons down the forearm. Adjust the length to make a slight train if desired. Line throughout.

See "The Wonderful 14th Century."

Drawings of interest:

p. 69 early sideless surcote
p. 70 Hairdressing - Women's
p. 76 Cut of Herjolsnes Cotehardie
p. 79 Later Sideless Surcote
p. 81 Typical Shoe (see also p. 127-128)
p. 80 Women's headressing

Making Placket under Lining

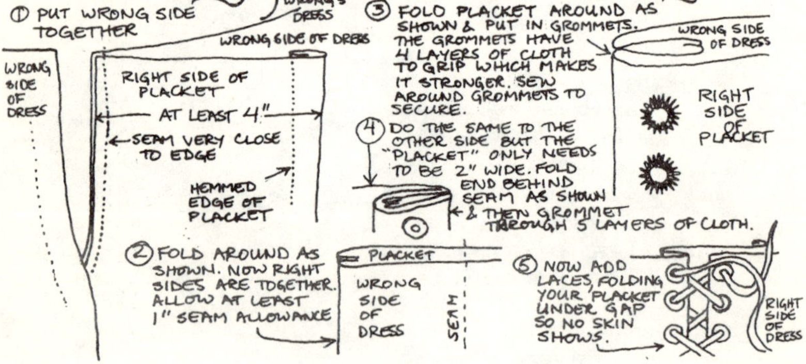

ALTERING THE MUNDANE PATTERN

The Sideless Surcoat

EITHER OF THESE CONSTRUCTIONS ARE PERIOD. SIDELESS SURCOATS WERE POPULAR WHEN COATHARDIES WERE FASHIONABLE.

(1) T-TUNIC CUT OR (2) CIRCULAR SKIRT CUT

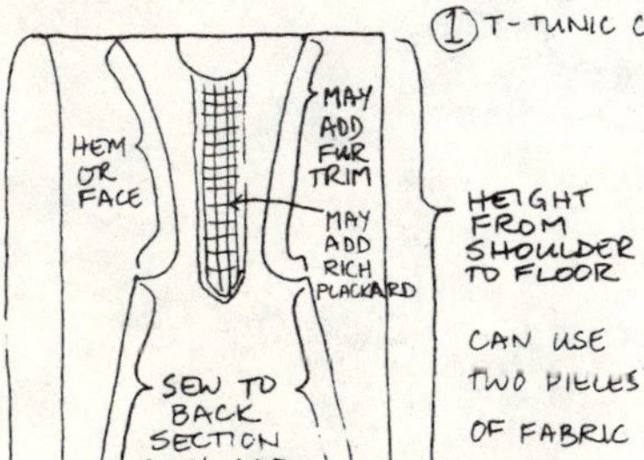

FINISH HEM

CAN USE TWO PIECES OF FABRIC INSTEAD OF FOLDING ONE.

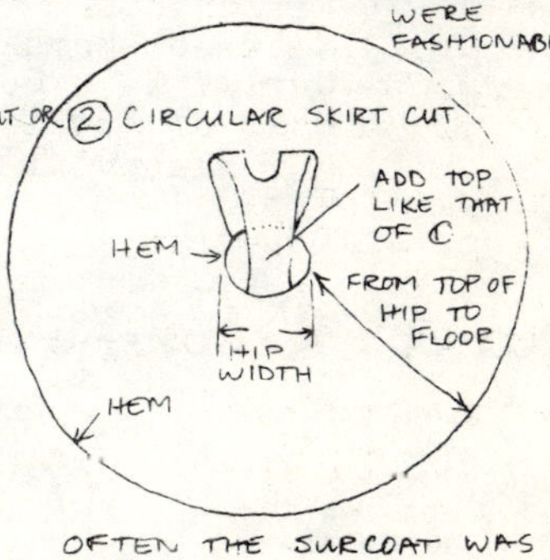

OFTEN THE SURCOAT WAS MORE THAN FLOOR LENGTH & NEEDED TO BE HELD UP IN ORDER TO WALK.

Lord's Cotehardie

For a lord's cotehardie or courtrepy, take any shirt pattern without a yoke or other decoration on the front and with a slit front neckline. One with a collar may help if you want to make a courtrepy, although you should try to find one with a stand-up round collar, not pointed. Cut the pattern in four pieces, counter-changing colors as desired if the cotehardie is parti-color. Lengthen the hem as you wish, although it can be almost as short as you want, and the most extreme versions were no longer than the shirt pattern will be. Set a line of buttons down the entire front center seam, with a line of hooks or snaps hidden underneath on a panel if you wish (the method of doing this is described in the chapter on this period). Add dagging at the hem if you wish. Fit tightly throughout; line throughout. Add padding between outside and lining if you want the most fashionable look, in the chest area. Adjust the sleeves to make them tight throughout and add a placket with button down the forearm, or make any of the sleeves for the courtrepy.

See "The Wonderful 14th Century".
Diagrams and Drawings of Interest:

- p. 68 The Chaperon
- p. 71 Period Hosen
- p. 73 Male Cotehardie
- p. 74 Cut of Male Cotehardie
- p. 76 Hair of Fashionable Man, also Courtrepy Neck
- p. 81 Typical Shoe - see also p. 127-128
- p. 82 Courtrepy

Parti-Coloring

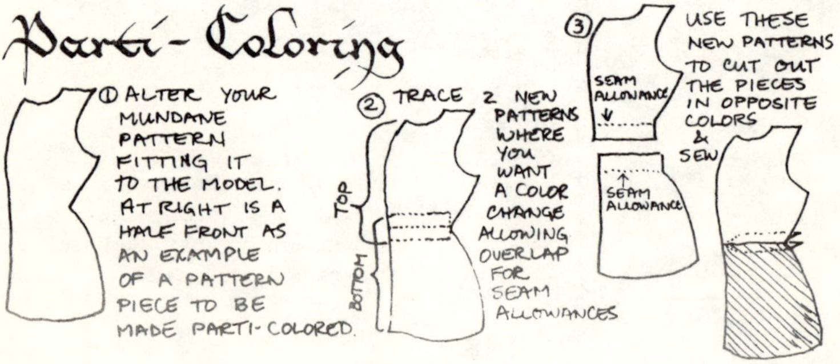

ALTERING A MUNDANE PATTERN

A Simple Shoe

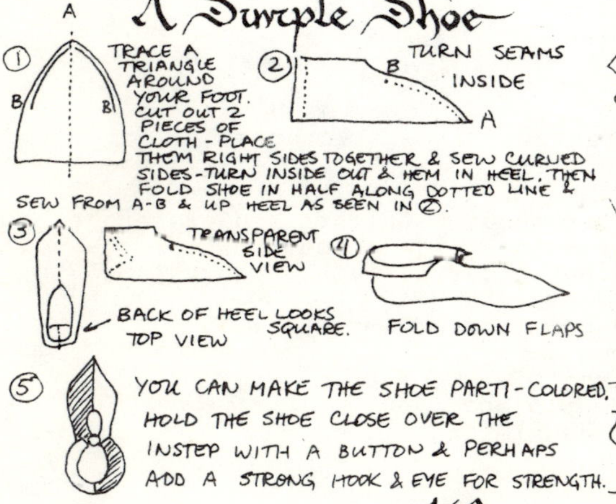

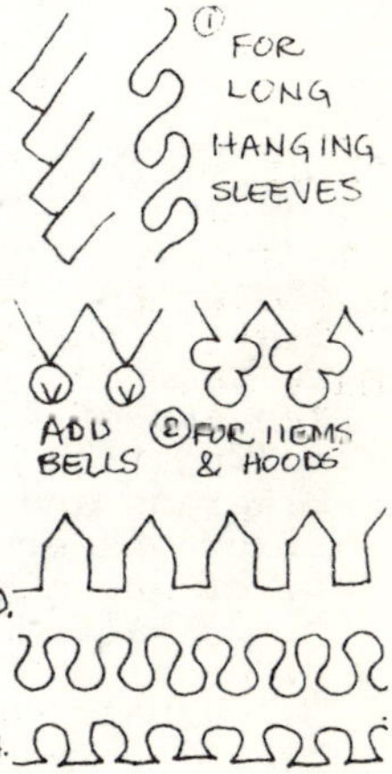

Lord's Houppelande Lady's

To make a lord's or lady's houppelande, take any mundane caftan pattern, with either a round stand-up collar or a flat pointed collar, depending on the style you want. Adapt the sleeve to resemble the shape in the picture (each sleeve will take about two yards, depending on the length you need). The curved section of the sleeve is sewn shut; the straight edge will be open from elbow level to the point. Put the lining in like a facing so that the open sleeve has a finished edge around it and the curved seam of the lining is turned with the finished side outward. Lay the wrong side of the sleeve against the wrong side of the lining, so that the right side is out on both inside and outside. Then sew the two sleeve pieces together at the shoulder to keep them together and even when put into the finished garment. Then sew the sleeve into the armhole in the usual way.

Extend the edge of the armhole on the body piece of the pattern to the width you want to make the garment very full. Be sure to extend the edge of the sleeve piece the same amount on each side at the armhole, so the two will match. Add gores at the side seams if you want yet more width. Extend the sides of the body piece to the full width of the fabric. Cut and sew as usual.

NOTE: The pattern pieces pictured here are Not to scale. Don't try to enlarge them and cut from them.

Start with your mundane pattern and exagerate to make the patterns look like those shown.

See end of "The Wonderful 14th Century" and all of "The 15th Century".

Diagrams and Drawings of interest:

p. 68 Chaperon
p. 81 See also 127-128, 160.
p. 83 Male Houpleland
p. 86 French Houpleland
p. 94 Hats
p. 159 Dags

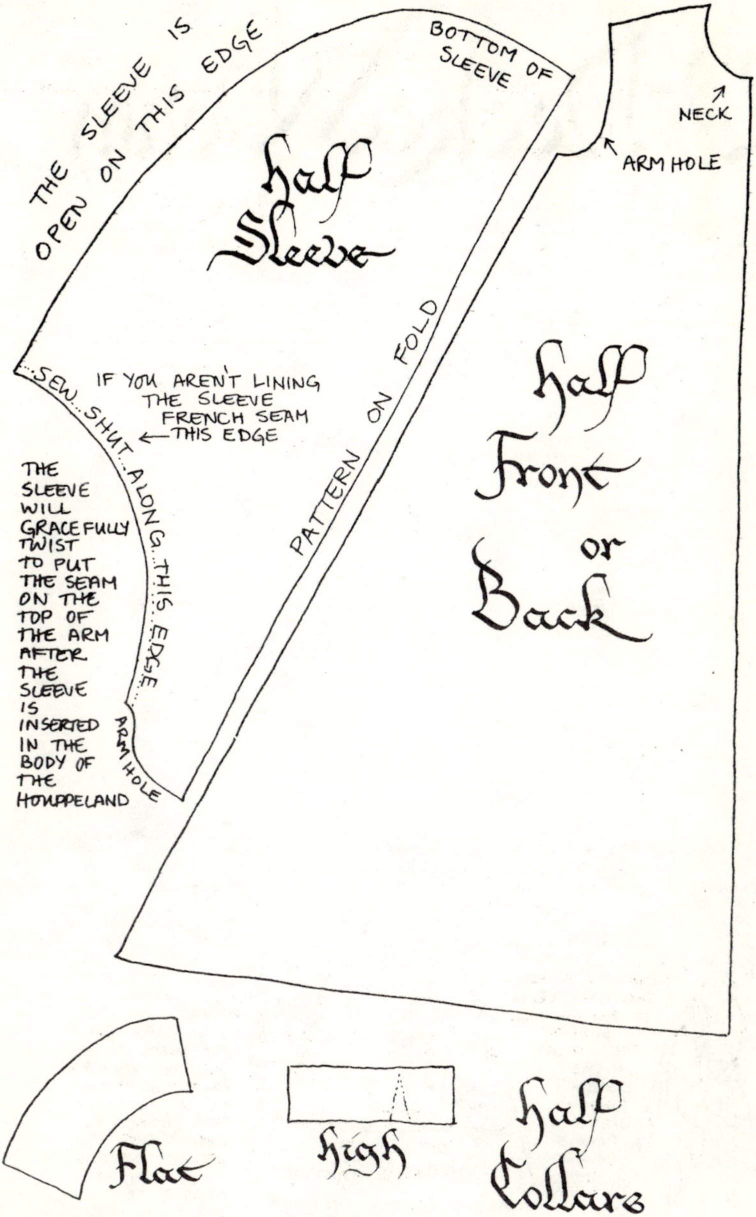
THE SLEEVE IS OPEN ON THIS EDGE
BOTTOM OF SLEEVE
Half Sleeve
NECK
ARM HOLE
IF YOU AREN'T LINING THE SLEEVE FRENCH SEAM THIS EDGE
SEW SHUT ALONG THIS EDGE
PATTERN ON FOLD
Half Front or Back
THE SLEEVE WILL GRACEFULLY TWIST TO PUT THE SEAM ON THE TOP OF THE ARM AFTER THE SLEEVE IS INSERTED IN THE BODY OF THE HOUPPELAND
ARM HOLE
Flat
High
Half Collars

V-Necked Gown

Find a mundane pattern in a bodice and skirt with the neckline in a straight V-shape, not crossed over. Make the skirt as full and long as desired with gores, etc. Add a stiff petticote to hold it out and give it a good line. Make both the back and front of the bodice V-shaped. Fold the edges of the front V at the center top, and of the back of the bodice at the zipper line, back until the V reaches the desired width to just come off the edge of the shoulder and meet at the center front and back at the lower hem. In other words, just fold the top of the V section back until it is as wide on top and as sharply angled as you want. Sew the front and back bodice to the skirt. Adjust the sleeves if necessary and add cuffs. Make the wide belt which fits just under the bust. If you wish, add the placket which fits in the lower part of the front V-section.

See Chapter "The 15th Century".

Diagrams and Drawings of Interest

p. 87 Square Collar Houpplande
p. 91 Women's Houppelande
p. 93 Round Dress
p. 95 Headdresses
p. 142 Top of Italian Sleeve

Italian Sleeve

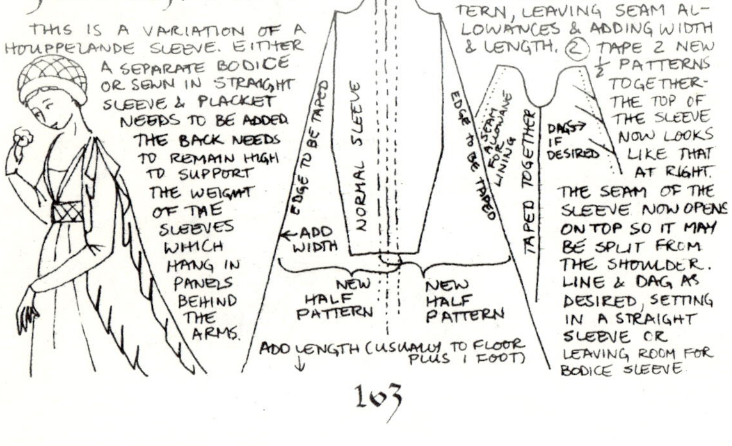

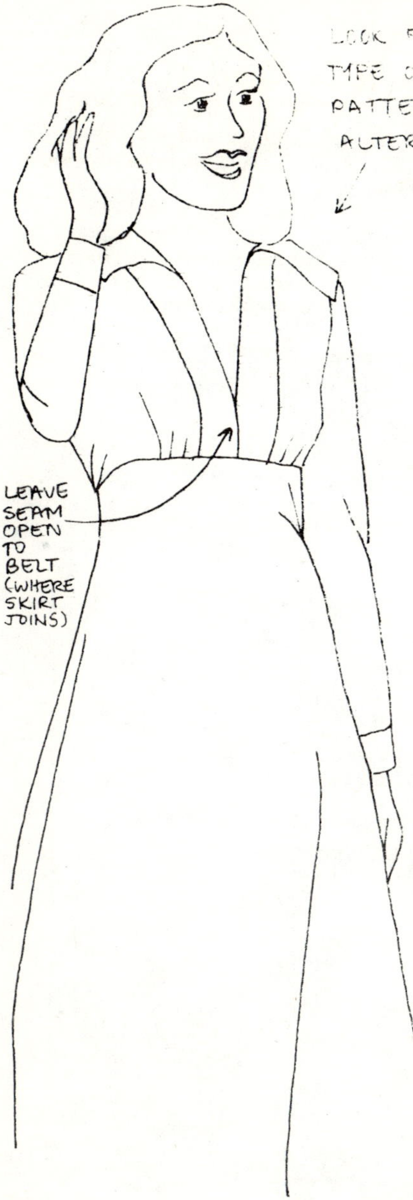

French Style c.1400

SKIRT WAS LESS FULL LIKE A COTE HARDIE OR MODERN PRINCESS STYLE CUT. IF YOU ARE ADDING HOUPPELANDE SLEEVES, LEAVE THE BACK HIGH, SO WEIGHT OF THE SLEEVES WON'T DRAG THE DRESS OFF YOUR SHOULDERS. YOU SHOULD MAKE A TIGHT SLEEVED LOW NECKED BODICE TO WEAR UNDER THE DRESS-OTHER WISE YOUR BARE FOREARM (SHUDDER) WILL SHOW. ALL THESE STYLES ARE HIGH-WAISTED.

Late 15th Century Male

To create either the long or the short pleated-front tunic, take a mundane caftan pattern. Slit the pattern into several lengthwise sections from top to bottom, making sure the edge of each slit is straight. Add a width of pattern paper between each slit equal to the depth of the pleat you want and pleat in the usual manner. Adjust the length and flare of the skirt as desired. Cut two pieces for each sleeve, the lining piece just like the pattern, the outer piece larger. Sew padding to the lining section at the shoulder to make the top of the sleeve as puffed as you want. Sew the two sections of the sleeve together, making sure the padding does not extend into the seam allowance on the shoulder. Sew to the body of the gown.

See "The 15th Century".
Diagrams of Interest
p. 90 The Gothic Man
p. 92 Look at Shoes
p. 94 Hats

Cloke Tunics & Variations

Several 15th and Early Male Tudor costumes were based on a circular cloke cut. These include the Cloke Tunic, the Journade and the Simar. The Simar can be made from a mundane bathrobe pattern but the diagram on page 103 is more authentic. Simply cut out a circular body of neccessary length leaving holes for neck and arm holes. Then set in sleeves-the type depends on which variation you are creating. Buy a mundane "peasant shirt" pattern with baggy sleeves of a tight sleeved shirt depending again on the style you are recreating.

See "The 15th Century" and "The Early Male Tudor Garb".

Diagrams of Interest.
p. 88 Cloke Tunic
p. 89 Male tunic
p. 92 The Journade
p. 101 The Simar, Shirt
p. 102 The Simar,
p. 103 Cut of Surcoat
p. 104 Riding Cloke
p. 113 Surcoat Diagram
p. 136 Right Figure

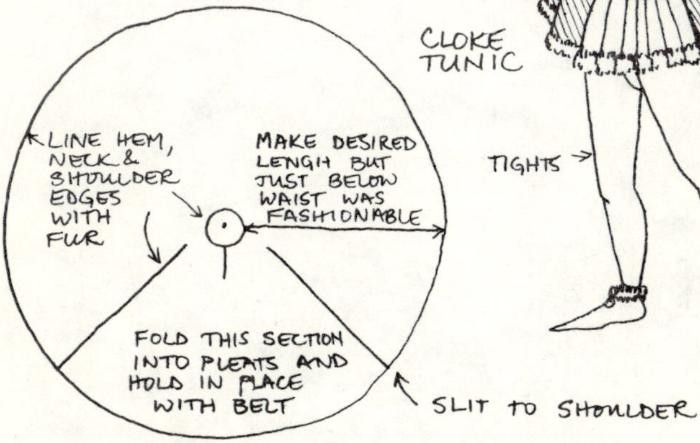

Pourpoint

For the pourpoint or Italian Renaissance style, take a mundane vest pattern. Widen the center V of the neckline to almost the waist. Add the plackard underneath or lacing across the opening. For the long undergarment, simply lengthen the bottom of the vest to about the knee, widening it enough to allow free movement. For bases, sew a very full pleated skirt to the bottom of the vest. For the Italian doublet, add a short pleated skirt to about hip level. Make sleeves from another pattern and lace to the armhole (the two upper sections do not have to match exactly, since the shirt should show between the sleeve and the arm section of the pourpoint.)

See Chapters on "Early Male Tudor Garb" and "A Note on Italian Renaissence Garb".

Drawings and Diagrams of interest:

p. 105 Bases
p. 106-7 Hats and Shoes
p. 108 Italian Bases
p. 111 Vest and Skirt
p. 114-116 Hats
p. 117 Shoe
p. 139 Pourpoint and tights with "Simar"

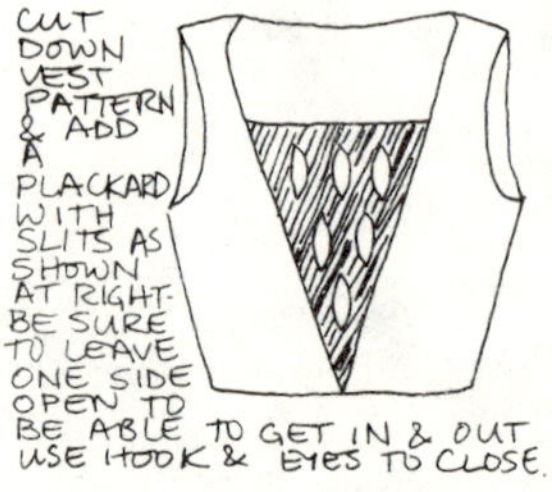

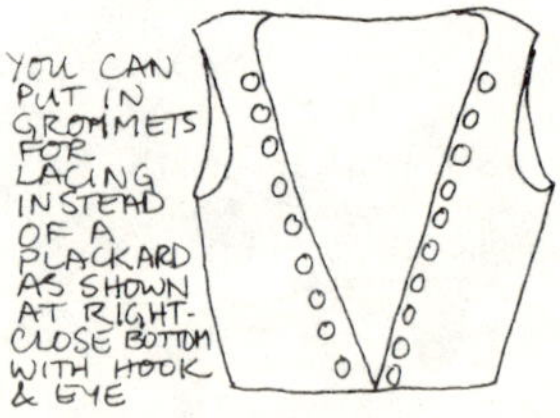

LACED POURPOINT WITH FAKED PUFFED SLEEVE

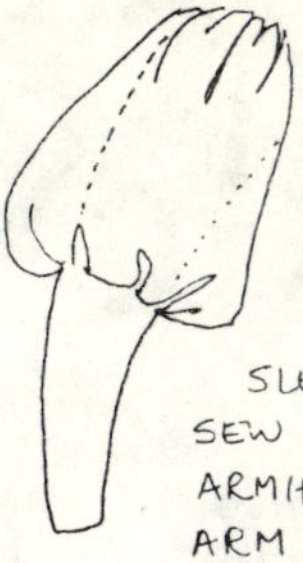

SOLID SLEEVE- A FULL SECTION SEWN OVER THE UPPER SECTION OF THE ARM AS SHOWN TO MAKE A SLIT PUFFED SLEEVE AS AT LEFT, SEW STRIPS FROM THE ARMHOLE TO THE LOWER ARM SECTION IF PUFFED SHIRT TO BE SEEN. OTHERWISE, CONSTRUCT STRIPS OVER AN UPPER SLEEVE AS SEEN ABOVE.

FULL SLEEVED SHIRT- PULL OUT PUFFS

TO MAKE SECTIONED SLEEVES, TAKE A NORMAL SLEEVE PATTERN LIKE THAT SHOWN AT LEFT - CUT IN HALF AT THE ELBOW AS SHOWN. CUT OUT & HEM OR FACE HOLES AND EDGES AND THEN PUT IN GROMMETS FOR FOR LACING. SEW TOP SECTION INTO TUBE; DO THE SAME WITH THE BOTTOM THEN LACE AS SHOWN.

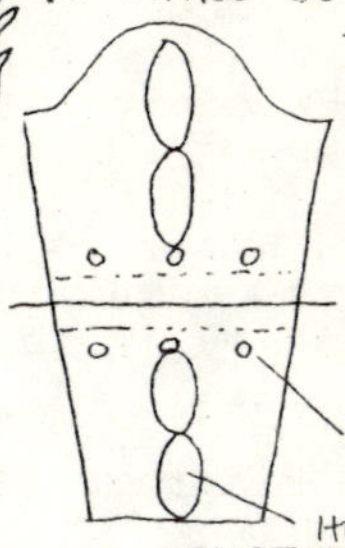

Henry VIII at the Field of Gold 1520

Female Tudor

To make a very fashionable Tudor you will have to cut the skirt and bodice in two parts, as described in the chapter on this period. The skirt will have to be adjusted to fit over the farthingale if it is used. For the shift, peasant Tudor style, or early Tudor of the time of Henry VII, this type of mundane pattern can be used. For a peasant style, slit the front center (the fold line of the pattern) down to the waist and add a line of lacing. Make the front of the shift bodice in one piece. For fashionable style, lower the square neckline in front, curving it up very slightly in the center front. Carry the bottom edge of the square out to almost the arm-pit and adjust the sides of the neckline to make it straight from shoulder to bottom of the square. The change in stress caused by this alteration may make a gusset necessary in the underarm. Adjust the sleeve as desired.

See the Chapter "Early Tudor Female Costume".
Drawings and Diagrams of Interest:

p. 122 Corset
p. 123 Farthingale
p. 125 High Necked Kirle and French Hood
p. 126 Sleeve cuts, Kirle, Gable
p. 128 Tudor Shoes
p. 129 English Hood
p. 130-131 Gable Hood Diagram
p. 132 Simple Hood

Peasant's Laced Front

NOTE THE CUT OF THE BODICE IS NOT AS EXTREME AS THE MORE FASHION-ABLE STYLE

NOTE THE BLOUSE WORN UNDER THIS PEASANT'S STYLE BODICE IS THE SAME AS THE MEN'S SHIRT WORN IN THIS PERIOD.

REMEMBER TO ADD EXTRA THICKNESSES OF CLOTH WHENEVER YOU ARE ADDING GROM-METS TO GIVE THEM ENOUGH TO GRIP. YOU ALSO NEED TO SEW AROUND METAL GROMMETS TO HOLD THEM IN PLACE.

Look for this style of mundane pattern to alter
NEED TO LENGTHEN THIS PATTERN TO DROP THE WAIST-LINE.
Fashionable Neckline

JEWELRY & BOOKS
from Raymond's Quiet Press
6336 LESLIE N.E.
ALBQ. N.M. 87109
Write for a
FREE CATALOG
Please include 25¢ for postage.
Besides our books, we now carry hand-crafted jewelry in gilt and natural bronze, including belt buckles, brooches & necklaces and hand enameled Pelicans & Laurels
The Great Roll of Arms of Atenveldt
The Pleasure Book
Raymond's Quiet Press
Medieval Costume
by Mistress Katrine de Baillie du Chat, O.L.
How to Cook Forsoothly
Champleve
Thor's hammer
Penannular brooches